VIDEO IN THE 80s

Emerging Uses for Television in Business, Education, Medicine and Government

Paula Dranov/Louise Moore/Adrienne Hickey

Knowledge Industry Publications, Inc.
White Plains, New York

The Video Bookshelf

Video in the 80s: Emerging Uses for Television in
Business, Education, Medicine and Government

Library of Congress Cataloging in Publication Data

Dranov, Paula.
  Video in the '80s.

  Includes index.
  1. Video recordings. I. Moore, Louise,
1952-   joint author. II. Hickey, Adrienne,
joint author. III. Title.
PN1992.95.D7   791.45'0973   80-15745
ISBN 0-914236-58-X

Printed in the United States of America

Contents

List of Tables

Structure and Size of the Market

The Video Users Survey

Business and Industry

Government

Medicine

Summary and Outlook

1

Introduction

Television has moved rapidly beyond its established role as an entertainment format to become a major communications tool for many organizations. When television is used to communicate internally—rather than to broadcast or cablecast to the public at large—it is called non-broadcast video. Also known as private television, institutional television and industrial television, nonbroadcast video constitutes a growing market for equipment and programming that should continue to expand in the foreseeable future. (Because there is no programming involved in television security systems, this nonbroadcast use of television is not considered video.)

INCREASING ACCEPTANCE OF VIDEO

One reason for the emergence of video as a communications medium is its cost effectiveness. This has been heightened by the energy crisis, which has contributed to sharply rising costs, particularly for transportation. Organizations with multiple locations or a need to reach geographically dispersed audiences have been forced to curtail personnel travel and to evaluate alternative means of communication. Distribution of a video program can often cut down or eliminate travel expenses—and also reduce costly personnel time—without sacrificing the visual impact of a face-to-face presentation.

A key factor in the cost effectiveness of video is the technology itself. In the past decade rapid advances have made better and better quality equipment available at increasingly lower prices. Easy-to-use cassette recorders and portable color cameras are now accessible to even the smallest potential video user. Newer developments in digital techniques, miniaturization, video disc technology and longitudinal video recording should continue to yield smaller, lighter weight, easier-to-use and less expensive equipment. (New technology and its implications will be discussed in Chapter 9.) As prices continue to drop while quality improves, video will be an even more cost-effective form of communication.

Of course, video is not the only alternative to more traditional communications methods. Video has gained acceptance in an environment of many new electronic forms of communication (e.g., online services, teletext and viewdata) at a time when the transfer of information has become even more important than in the past. Although video is not appropriate for every purpose, in many situations the visual element is crucial and video is clearly the best alternative. Such areas as employee training, presentation of new product information to a widely scattered sales staff, and continuing professional education courses are among the most obvious cases. In addition to the benefit of visual impact, video may also offer the advantages of consistency of presentation and flexibility of scheduling, enabling all viewers to receive the same information but at times appropriate to their own needs.

Moreover, the generations now coming into adulthood have grown up with television and appear better able to absorb information through this medium than through traditional print formats. As video is applied more and more in education, business, medicine, etc., its use is becoming a necessity rather than just a possibility. And as people become comfortable with the idea of using television and with the equipment itself, they are more likely to find exciting new applications for video, such as the remote medical diagnosis described in Chapter 7. This is beginning to happen in other market segments as well, with long-established users finding new ways to expand video services. More important at the moment, however, is the fact that increasing numbers of organizations are using video.

There are several relatively distinct categories of nonbroadcast video users, including business and industrial firms, educational institutions, medical institutions, government agencies, and religious and other non-profit organizations. Of course, some overlap exists among these markets. For instance, a medical school could be considered either medical or educational, while a veterans' hospital might be called either medical or government. Each of these groups uses video in unique ways, as well as in ways common to other segments. An organization may produce its own programs, rent or purchase prerecorded programs to play back on its own equipment, or both.

VIDEO EQUIPMENT

What all users have in common is one or more video recorders/players. Some organizations may have networks of thousands of locations equipped to play back programs while others have only a few. Considerable variety in types of players available has developed; the type used often depends on whether the user is producing his/her own programs, and on the amount and quality of the programming needed. Similarly, among users who produce programming, the number and types of cameras used and how elaborate a production facility has been assembled will vary from one institution to another. The following pages provide a brief summary of the kinds of equipment being used in the nonbroadcast video market.

Video Recorders

Video recording became technically feasible in 1956 when the Ampex Corp. introduced the first video tape recorder (VTR). This system was called the quadraplex format, meaning that four separate video heads were used to record on 2-inch-wide video tape. Very large and very expensive, the system could only be used effectively by commercial broadcasters or large business organizations. The quadraplex format remains the broadcast quality standard.

Over the following decade, technological advances reduced both the size and cost of VTRs. In 1967 a totally new type of video tape recorder, called a helical VTR, was introduced. Helical equipment, which uses only one or two recording heads, was developed as an alternative for institutional users who could not afford quadraplex equipment. A helical VTR is also smaller and easier to use. Within the helical category, however, there are several totally different tape formats, varying both in size and track configuration. The early helical VTRs were 1-inch and ½-inch; ¾-inch and ¼-inch were added later. Usually, the larger the tape size, the better the recording quality.

One problem often associated with video is the incompatibility of tape sizes and formats. Video playback units can accommodate only one size of tape; i.e., a program recorded on one size cannot be played back on another. Furthermore, differences in the recording or track configuration can make even tapes of the same width incompatible, thus multiplying the types of recorders and players in use.

Early helical VTRs were reel-to-reel machines, but in 1969, Sony developed a video cassette format—the ¾-inch U-Matic. Once the U-Matic cassette player went on sale in 1972, it was quickly adopted by business and government organizations attracted by its simplicity, compactness, good picture quality and reasonable price. The use of a cassette eliminated the handling and threading of video tape, an appealing feature for inexperienced institutional users. Although other manufacturers have since produced their own ¾-inch video cassette recorders (VCRs), the advantage of the U-Matic format is that all machines are compatible; in other words, a ¾-inch cassette recorded on one machine can be played back on any other.

This compatibility is not a feature of a newer, popular cassette size, ½-inch. These VCRs became widely available after 1975 with a number of manufacturers entering the market. Although ½-inch recorders were aimed at the developing home video market, more durable and expensive models have been introduced for institutional users. However, there are two different ½-inch formats—Beta and VHS—and they are incompatible.

Both the ¾-inch and ½-inch cassette recorders were designed to be distribution formats, meaning they would play back programs that were produced on film or using expensive quad recorders. In response to demand from the market, manufacturers began introducing editing and production models in the ¾-inch and ½-inch formats, thus facilitating the production of original programming using this equipment. Nevertheless, the largest nonbroadcast video users have either stayed with 2-inch quad recorders, or adopted one of the several 1-inch helical recorders developed as production units. In general, the 1-inch VTRs are less costly than quad, and are smaller and more portable. At present, there are two main, incompatible versions of the 1-inch VTR — Type B and Type C — which differ in their tape threading and recording technology.

Video Cameras

Video cameras can be broadly classified as either studio or portable. Although studio cameras are also used in the field, they are heavy and must be mounted to a tripod or pedestal. Portable cameras can be hand-held or shoulder-mounted, and often operate on battery power. Within each type, there is a wide variety of price and quality. Studio cameras, for example, range from a $3500 simple, "no frills" model to a high quality production camera in the $50,000 to $100,000 category—the type found in most broadcast studio operations. The higher quality shoulder-mounted portable cameras can be used for electronic field production (EFP) of programming, as well as for electronic news gathering (ENG) — for which many portable cameras were first developed. The type and quality of camera selected depends on the type and amount of programming to be produced. Established users who produce a large number of programs and/or who need high quality programs may have many cameras of different types, including some of broadcast quality. A very small video operation, on the other hand, may call for one simple portable camera.

Of course, a basic choice that affects price is between color and black-and-white cameras. It is the camera and not the video tape that determines whether a program is in color or black-and-white. Through the early 1970s color cameras were so much more expensive than black-and-white that price was the chief factor in the decision. In the late 1970s, however, the price of color cameras dropped sharply, and the decision can now be based primarily on other factors. A color camera, for example, is often more complex to use and requires a higher level of lighting than a black-and-white camera. A potential user must consider whether color will make a difference in the particular programs to be produced. Color would be advantageous in a sales/marketing tape, for example, but might be superfluous in a taped lecture.

Editing Equipment

There are three basic types of editing equipment: manual, control track and computerized SMPTE* time code editing. In the early days of video, editing involved the actual cutting and splicing of the tape, an unsatisfactory procedure that limited the reuse of the tape, clogged video heads and often produced a "glitch," or loss of picture, at the splice.

Today's manual editing systems involve transferring scenes electronnically from one tape to another using two VTRs. One machine plays the production tape while the other records selected scenes onto a blank master edit tape. Because the two machines are not locked together electronically, this process lacks precision — edits are not always smooth because the cut depends on split-second timing on the part of the person doing the machine editing.

Control track editing electronically controls the timing of the edit. The electronics read a series of synchronizing pulses on the edge of the tape and lock the two VTRs together. When they are rolled back, the machines are completely synchronized and the record function switches on automatically at a pre-set edit point.

Computerized editing makes use of a standardized SMPTE time code which is recorded on one of the audio tracks on the tape and displayed on the video screen. The time code assigns an eight-digit number that refers to

---

*SMPTE stands for Society of Motion Picture and Television Engineers, the professional association which developed the code standards.

the hour, minute, second and frame of the tape. A computer can then be programmed to respond to specific frame numbers and automatically perform the edit to perfect frame accuracy. Computer editing is the fastest and most precise system — and, the most expensive.

Other Equipment

Depending on the sophistication of the video operation, other production equipment may be needed. There may be a control room with a production switcher, the equipment that allows the director or technical director to choose from several camera shots and/or video playbacks, film or slides. The director may also work with a special effects generator that can combine several sources and change the pictures's shape and size to create a totally different image.

In addition, lighting and audio needs vary according to the extent of video use and the complexity of the production facility.

VIDEO SERVICES

Applications of video range from employee training to elementary school productions. Well established as a training tool, the medium is being used increasingly by corporations for sales and marketing, public relations, management information and employee motivational purposes. Colleges and universities are presenting entire courses on video tape; elementary and secondary schools are using prerecorded programming as supplementary instructional materials and, in some cases, producing their own programs. Governmental agencies, particularly at the federal level, are applying video for instructional and informational purposes. In medicine it has proven clearly valuable for both student instruction and continuing professional education. Nonprofit organizations are also discovering the usefulness of video, particularly in educational and fund-raising activities.

These and other video applications will be discussed in greater detail in subsequent chapters. A cautionary note is in order, however: video is not right for every organization, nor for every potential application within that organization.

There is no general rule of thumb on whether an organization should turn to video. Some of the questions to be considered are: What are the potential applications within the organization? What are the specific advantages of television for each of them? What are the alternatives to television for each application? Is video the most cost-effective way to meet these needs? Obviously, the answers to these questions will vary from organization to organization. The general advantages of video have already been noted. These include the effectiveness of visual impact, consistency of presentation and scheduling flexibility. In many situations, these benefits will result in a considerable cost savings.

The lack of careful planning and analysis before making a financial investment in video is the most frequent error made by new users. Closely related, however, is the naiveté with which such users frequently approach the technical aspects of production and the acquisition of hardware. Production of professional-quality video programming is not an effortless undertaking. It requires more than a crash course in how to operate a camera.

Further, managers may have some unrealistic expectations of what video can and cannot accomplish. A frequent complaint on the part of video staffs is the lack of appreciation among managers and other departments in the organization for the technical considerations involved in producing television programming. Conflicts often arise because of demands for "overnight" production and the necessity for giving one project priority over another. Pressures on video departments can be compounded when the staff has responsibility for other A/V materials and productions.

Video Staffs

The size and background of video staffs vary from organization to organization. Television may be the responsibility of a single person or of a full-fledged department with a staff of producers, engineers, writers and other creative and technical personnel. Often, it is merely the extension of an already-existing audiovisual department and draws upon resources and personnel already in place. An A/V department with film production capability may be able to smoothly incorporate television into its activities. Frequently, these departments respond to the programming requests of "clients" elsewhere in the parent organization by supplying the creative and technical skills. Then, too, because video is so frequently used for training, responsibility may be vested in training or personnel departments.

In many cases, television becomes the responsibility of a manager who has come up through the ranks of an organization and is well acquainted with all aspects of its operations. All too often, of course, this type of manager lacks expertise in the technical side of video. On the other hand, a video professional with the requisite technical expertise may lack an understanding of the organization and its unique needs and may fail because he or she has no "feel" for the organization itself. The fact that video staffs frequently grow out of pre-existing audiovisual departments to some extent overcomes this "either-or" dilemma, although some may not adapt as readily as others to television production and programming.

Nonbroadcast television is opening up a large, new job market for the graduates of some 1200 college and university film and television programs. While most of these graduates have broadcast television ambitions, there are simply not enough broadcast jobs to accommodate them all. As an alternative, many are starting out in nonbroadcast video departments in hopes of acquiring enough professional experience to move on eventually into the broadcast sphere.

The expansion of the nonbroadcast market also has attracted video professionals who started out in broadcast television and made the switch for higher salaries, more professional responsibility or, perhaps, greater opportunities for advancement than they might otherwise expect. Then, too, in communications centers like New York and Los Angeles, freelance producers, directors, writers and other creative and technical personnel may move with ease back and forth between broadcast and nonbroadcast television.

ABOUT THIS BOOK

Video in the 80s is intended as a guide for established, new and potential users of video, as well as for manufacturers, publishers and distributors of video equipment and programming. It provides information on how video is being used in each market segment and on the prospects for its use in the coming decade. Much of the statistical data included is based on a nationwide survey of nearly 1100 video users, conducted by Knowledge Industry Publications. This information is supplemented by an overview of each user group and by case studies of selected organizations actively engaged in video.

Chapter 2 analyzes the size and structure of the nonbroadcast video market. Chapters 3 through 8 explore video use in business and industry, education, medicine, government and nonprofit organizations. The final chapter offers some thoughts on how video will work for institutional users as the 1980s unfold.

2

Structure and Size of the Market

In addition to users, the participants in the nonbroadcast video market are manufacturers, dealers, video publishers (producers of proprietary programs), consultants and production houses. Most companies in these groups also serve either the broadcast television or consumer video markets or both. Rapid growth in the nonbroadcast arena over the past decade and the potential for continued expansion make this an attractive and important market for these suppliers, whose numbers have swelled along with the market.

STRUCTURE OF THE MARKET

Manufacturers

Virtually every manufacturer of television viewing and production equipment and related accessories is involved to some extent in the nonbroadcast market. These companies range from large manufacturers of broadcast quality equipment, such as Ampex, IVC and RCA, who supply products to more sophisticated users, to the smallest accessory supplier. Although there are more than 200 manufacturers competing for a share of nonbroadcast equipment sales, the field has long been dominated by a handful of companies that have actively developed this market, including Sony, JVC and Panasonic. Such companies offer a full range of cameras, VTRs, production equipment and television receivers. (For a complete listing of manufacturers serving the nonbroadcast video market, see Appendix C.)

While video hardware manufacturers realize that the nonbroadcast market is important to their business, most have no clear picture of what proportion of their sales comes from this area. This is mainly because equipment sales to most users are made by video dealers. For the most part, manufacturers have direct contact only with large customers making bulk equipment purchases. As a result, manufacturers are largely unaware of exactly how organizations are using video and what specific needs they have.

Dealers

Since nearly all users purchase at least some equipment from video dealers, their role in this market is an important one. There are approximately 500 dealers in the United States, and a number of them have multiple branch locations throughout a region. Most dealerships are local and privately owned, but some are divisions of other companies, e.g., video manufacturers or production houses. Because dealers often carry a full line of audio and film products as well as video, and may also serve broadcast and consumer markets, it is no easier to assess the nonbroadcast market at this level, particularly given the geographic dispersion of the dealers and the customers they serve.

It is usually the dealer to whom an organization turns when venturing into video. Regardless of the kind of programming the new user may plan to distribute — often a prerecorded or custom-produced program — it will still be necessary to acquire VTRs. As a user moves into production, or steps up to more complex, better quality equipment, it is often the dealer who provides the information, guidance and instruction. Many dealers rent equipment as well as sell it. Some also provide production services, such as editing, dubbing and duplicating, thereby also qualifying as production houses.

Production Houses

Commercial production houses, which number about 500 in the United States, offer video users a wide range of services. Some are really only post-production houses that will edit a tape, transfer programs to a different format if necessary and/or duplicate tapes. Even those users who are heavily involved in production are usually not equipped to duplicate video tape in quantity for distribution to large networks, so duplication is the most frequently provided service.

Other production houses are involved in every aspect of production from planning to directing and shooting to post-production. They may offer their own studio and/or mobile facilities to go to the organization itself or to a remote location. Production houses handle a variety of video programming from simple to elaborate.

Consultants

Consultants, who may occasionally be part of full-service production houses, offer the creative expertise often needed by inexperienced video users. Management in a business or hospital, for example, may call in a consultant and simply present the communications problem it is facing. The consultant will work with the organization to develop a program concept and will then follow through with scripting and production planning. If equipped, the consultant will carry out the production; if not, a good production house will be enlisted to produce the custom program.

Consultants may also be called upon to design and implement the installation of a video facility, as well as training of the personnel who will be using it. Other consultant services include feasibility studies on video and evaluations of existing or proposed facilities or programming.

Publishers

Video publishers produce and sell off-the-shelf programs primarily to business and educational organizations. Many of these customers have their own players but no facilities to produce programming, although packaged programming is also used by organizations with their own production facilities.

There are more than 100 video publishers providing programming to the nonbroadcast market. In addition to commercial publishers, some professional associations, colleges and universities, and medical institutions publish and distribute their own programming both by rental and sale. Long-time leading publishers in this market are Deltak, Advanced Systems, Inc. and Time-Life Video.

Again, many of these publishers serve the consumer market as well as nonbroadcast users. While consumers are more likely to select entertainment programming, however, nonbroadcast users are most likely to choose training and education applications. As later chapters will illustrate, packaged programming is used most often for student instruction, medical education, continuing education and employee training.

Users

As noted in Chapter 1, nonbroadcast video users can be divided into five major groups: business/industry, medicine, education, government and nonprofit organizations. Attempts to quantify each segment and thus to arrive at the total number of users are fraught with difficulties. Neither manufacturers nor dealers can identify all nonbroadcast users nationally on the basis of equipment sales, and the issue is further complicated by the fact that some users rent equipment or acquire it second-hand.

Previous estimates of the scope of the market were made by Judith M. and Douglas P. Brush in two separate reports, *Private Television Communications: A Report to Management* (Knowledge Industry Publications, Inc., 1974) and *Private Television Communications: An Awakening Giant* (International Industrial Television Association, 1977). In the first study, the Brushes placed the number of organizations using video at more than 300; in the second, they reported that the ranks had been swelling by nearly 30% annually, implying a total of approximately 700 or more users. However, these estimates dealt only with corporate and some government networks and were based on the assumption that only very large, geographically dispersed organizations could afford to invest in video.

As video has gained in acceptance and the technology has become more accessible (see Chapter 1), smaller organizations of every type have begun to use it. Many, of course, start out with only one or two programs and a limited number of playback locations. At the same time, it can be assumed that even more of the large, geographically dispersed organizations are using video. Advanced Systems, Inc., one of the largest publishers of video training programs, claims that its customer base includes 90% of the *Fortune* 1000. A large northeastern dealer estimates that the total number of users nationwide may be 80,000 to 100,000, but this huge number must include many thousands of marginal users.

Of course, not every organization with one video cassette player should be considered a video user. For the purpose of this study, a video user is defined as an organization that is *actively* engaged in communicating information to its members, customers or other wider constituencies by the systematic selection or creation of video programs. By this definition, the training department that buys one prerecorded program is not a video user, but the bank that creates its own community news show to present in several branches is, even if the production is done by a free-lance cameraman working with portapak equipment. Similarly, an organization that rents equipment, produces a single program and then abandons video, is not considered a user; a school district that purchases prerecorded tapes and regularly distributes them to six elementary schools for classroom viewing is considered a user.

More specifically, a user is an organization that has more than one playback location, or that produces its own programs and/or has its own studio. By this definition, nonbroadcast users probably number about 27,000 in 1980.

Of this number, business/industrial firms constitute half, or about

13,500. There are an estimated 5000 educational users, representing roughly 19%, of the total; about 60% of these are school systems and 40% are institutions of higher education. Another 5000 users, or 19%, are in the field of medicine, and approximately 3000 government users account for 11% of the total. Nonprofit organizations that use video number about 800, or 2% of the total. (See Table 2.1.)

Table 2.1: Nonbroadcast Video Users, 1980

Type of Organization	Number of Users
Business/industry	13,500
Educational	5,000
Medical	5,000
Government	3,000
Nonprofit	800
Total	27,000

Source: Knowledge Industry Publications, Inc. estimates.

SIZE OF THE MARKET

The overlap among the nonbroadcast market and the broadcast television and consumer video markets presents the same difficulties assessing total expenditures as it does with the number of users, particularly since the majority of users are producing their own progamming. In-house production incurs overhead and salary costs, as well as per-program expenses for such needs as supplies, duplication, outside talent, etc. These internal expenditures are especially hard to quantify because video operations are often contained within a media or A/V department, which also produces in other media, or within a training, education or public relations department where video budgets are not segregated.

However, based on the results of the *Video Register* survey (see Chapter 3), import figures on video equipment, and previous estimates of market size, it can be estimated that 1980 expenditures for nonbroadcast video will total $1.1 billion, reflecting a compound annual growth rate of 28% since the Brush estimate of $413 million for 1976. As Table 2.2 illustrates, this impressive total includes $400 million for equipment, $60 million for the purchase or rental of packaged programs, $550 million for in-house production and $90 million for outside production and services.

Table 2.2: U.S. Nonbroadcast Video Expenditures, 1980
(in millions)

Kind of Expenditure		Amount
Equipment		$400
Programming (total)		700
In-house production (including salaries, overhead, out-of-pocket expenses)	550	
Outside production and and services	90	
Packaged programming	60	
Total		1,100

Source: Knowledge Industry Publications, Inc. estimates.

Some perspective on this activity is provided in Table 2.3, where nonbroadcast video expenditures are compared to selected other categories of video expenditures. Total apparent sales of TV and radio broadcast equipment will reach $1056 million in 1980, based on Commerce

Table 2.3: Trends in Video Expenditures, 1974-80
(in millions)

Expenditure	1974	1978	1979	1980
TV & radio broadcast equipment[1]	794	724	945	1,056
Nonbroadcast equipment	117	240	350	400
Nonbroadcast programming[2]	166	500	600	700
Total	283	740	950	1,100
Consumer equipment (VCRs and cameras)[3]	NA	325	420	491
Consumer programming (blank and prerecorded tape)	NA	114	213	256
Total		439	633	747

[1]Total of domestic product shipments and net imports; 1980 projection assumes 1979 level of imports/exports.
[2]Includes in-house, custom and prerecorded programming. In-house expenditures include salaries, overhead and per-program costs.
[3]Estimates from *Home Video Report* (Knowledge Industry Publications, Inc.), January 7, 1980.
Sources: U.S. Department of Commerce; Knowledge Industry Publications, Inc.

Department estimates. Undoubtedly, a significant portion of that total is actually destined for nonbroadcast use. Similarly, some portion of consumer equipment sales, estimated at $491 million in 1980 by *Home Video Report* newsletter, can be attributed to the nonbroadcast market. Estimates of expenditures for programming indicate that nonbroadcast video users are spending nearly three times as much as are home video users; home users, of course, incur no significant expenses for overhead.

It can also be estimated that, although they represent 50% of the total number of users, business and industrial users account for about 60% of total spending in this market, or $660 million. Educational spending probably constitutes 15% of the total, or $165 million, and government accounts for 12%, or $132 million. Medical institutions will spend $110 million on video, or 10% of the total, and nonprofit organizations 3%, or $33 million. (See Table 2.4.)

Table 2.4: Nonbroadcast Expenditures by User Segment (in millions)

Segment	Amount	% of Total
Business/industry	$ 660	60%
Education	165	15
Government	132	12
Medicine	110	10
Nonprofit	33	3
Total	1,100	100

Source: Knowledge Industry Publications, Inc. estimates.

Although the total of $1.1 billion yields an average annual user expenditure of nearly $41,000, it must be remembered that there is a wide range of expenditure levels in this market. While some users are spending more than $1 million on video, the majority are probably spending less than $100,000 and many, only a few thousand dollars per year.

In addition to the range in total spending, there are considerable differences in levels of program production and purchases of equipment and published programming. The following chapters will illustrate these differences by user segment.

3

The Video Users Survey

A total of 1087 organizations responded to the nationwide survey of nonbroadcast video users conducted by Knowledge Industry Publications, Inc. in the summer of 1979.

Among the respondents were 463 business/industrial firms, 393 educational institutions, 92 government agencies, 81 medical institutions and 44 religious and other nonprofit organizations.

The survey elicited a wide range of information on how video is being used at the start of the 1980s and the outlook for its use during the next five years. It considered several aspects of nonbroadcast video that had never been adequately treated before. These include: the specific uses of video; the organization of video facilities; the size of video networks; the type and value of the hardware in use; the amount of programming produced, purchased and rented; and the budgets under which video units operate.

METHODOLOGY

The survey was conducted in connection with the publication of the 1979-80 edition of *The Video Register,* a Knowledge Industry Publications directory of manufacturers, dealers, publishers, services and nonbroadcast users. *The Video Register* is the most complete listing available of major video users in the fields of business/industry, government, education, medicine, religion and nonprofit institutions. As an incentive to complete the questionnaire, respondents were offered a free copy of *The Video Register*; they were also guaranteed confidentiality.

A total of 5050 questionnaires were mailed to the 1050 users listed in the 1978-79 edition of *The Video Register*, as well as to 4000 prospects culled from various mailing lists and lists of trade show attendees. Responses were received from approximately 900 organizations. A subsequent telephone follow-up of both nonrespondents and other organizations deemed likely users by the survey staff raised the total to 1087. Thus, the response rate was 22%. (Some additional responses were received too late to tabulate and others were missing so much information that they were not included.)

Not all respondents completed the entire two-page questionnaire. Some users answered only the first page of questions; others simply skipped those questions that could not be readily answered. These omissions applied particularly to questions on budgets. Therefore, some of the data presented in this report are calculated on a base of 852, instead of 1087.

Prior to tabulation, a number of users were selected at random from each of the five main categories to be contacted for the case studies that appear in subsequent chapters. These users were contacted by telephone and asked if they would waive the confidentiality, and were asked for additional information not requested in the questionnaire.

Tabulation

Results were reported for each question both numerically and as a percentage of the total respondents in the group. Responses were separated by market category: business/industry, government, education, medicine, and religious and other nonprofit institutions. A sixth ("other") group of 14 respondents was unclassified. Some of the different video markets were then broken down into even smaller segments. For example, the category broadly defined as business/industry was subdivided into industry/manufacturing, banking, insurance, other financial services, wholesale/retail organizations, utilities, transportation, communications and service industries.

In analyzing the results for this survey, these nine business segments were regrouped as follows: industry/manufacturing; financial (including insurance companies, banks and other financial firms); and service industries (including wholesale/retail firms, utilities, transportation companies, communications companies, and other service organizations). The education, government and medical markets and the nonprofit category were considered separately.

Table 3.1 shows the number of respondents in each category and the percentage of the survey sample each group represents.

Table: 3.1: Respondents to *Video Register* Survey of Video Users

Kind of Organization	No. of Respondents	Percent of Sample
Total business/industry	463	42.5%
Manufacturing/industrial firms	239	22.0
Financial firms	70	6.4
Banking	11	1.0%
Insurance	37	3.4
Other financial	22	2.0
Service industry firms	154	14.1
Wholesale/retail	46	4.2
Utility	51	4.7
Transportation	8	0.7
Communications	28	2.6
Other service industry	21	1.9
Educational institutions	393	36.1
Medical institutions	81	7.4
Government	92	8.5
Religious/other nonprofit	44	4.0
Unclassified	14	1.3
Total	1087	100.0

As Table 3.1 indicates, 42.5% of the replies tabulated fell into the broad category of business/industry, while 36.1% constituted the education segment, 8.5% the government segment, 7.4% the medical segment and 4.0% the nonprofit segment (including religious institutions).

Compared to the market breakdown given in Chapter 2, where educational users were estimated as 17% of all users, it would appear that the education segment is greatly over-represented in the survey, thus distorting the proportions of the other segments. There are several possible reasons for this exaggeration. First, educational users tend to be more visible than do users in other segments; the universe of potential users is relatively small and easily defined. These users also tend to participate frequently in seminars, conferences, trade shows, etc., so are likely to appear on lists of known users. Further, educational organizations tend to be more willing to be identified as users, thus encouraging an onslaught of questionaries, promotional materials, etc., unlike many of their counterparts in other segments, particularly business/industry. It is also possible that educational users are more survey-oriented and therefore more willing to answer questionnaires.

The 42.5% of survey responses classified as business/industry accurately reflects the fact that this market segment is the largest, although the proportion should be somewhat higher. Similarly, the government and medical segments appear smaller in the survey than they actually are because the education group is so large. Moreover, the medical segment, which appears smaller than government in the survey, is larger in reality.

Market Representation

The obvious question about the *Video Register* survey is how large a proportion of the actual nonbroadcast market it represents. Based on the estimates of the number of users in each segment given in Chapter 2, the percentage of the total number of users represented by the survey is roughly 4%. Survey respondents in the business/industry segment constitute about 3% of total corporate users, while those in the medical segment represent nearly 2% of all medical users. Educational users who answered the survey account for about 8% of all users in this segment, again an unusually high proportion. The nonprofit respondents represent about 5% of that segment and government respondents, 3%.

Although the percentages represented in the survey may not appear very high, it can be assumed that those included in the survey are among the most active video users. They are likely to be the largest, most experienced users — those who participate in trade shows, subscribe to trade publications, attend conferences, and, in general, keep up with technological advances in the field. They are also more likely to be spending more money on equipment and production and thus account for a much larger proportion of market expenditures than their sheer numbers would indicate.

SUMMARY OF FINDINGS

Following is a brief summary of responses to survey questions on facilities and equipment, personnel, programming and budgets. Further information will be presented in subsequent chapters on the individual market segments.

Facilities and Equipment

The majority of all users—just over 60%—reported having between one and 25 playback locations, with 40.2% listing between one and 10. Only 11.3% reported a network of more than 100 playback locations. Table 3.2 shows the number of playback locations operated by the various user groups.

Table 3.2: Size of Video Network

No. Playback Locations	All Users (N=1087)[1]	Business/Industry (N=463)	Education (N=393)	Government (N=92)	Medical (N=81)	Nonprofit (N=44)
			Percentage of Users			
1-10	40.2%	29.8%	45.8%	48.9%	59.3%	52.3%
11-25	21.2	23.5	21.4	16.3	16.0	18.2
26-50	11.1	12.3	8.9	20.7	7.4	4.5
51-100	8.8	12.1	7.9	4.3	3.7	2.3
101-300	8.6	13.0	5.6	5.4	2.5	4.5
Over 300	2.7	2.8	2.0	—	3.7	4.5
Unspecified	0.9	1.1	0.5	—	—	4.5
No answer	6.5	5.4	7.9	4.3	7.4	9.1

[1]Includes 14 unclassified respondents.

The most popular format, by far, was the ¾-inch VTR, used by 57.3% of all respondents. However, 41.7% reported using ½-inch machines while nearly 10% employed other formats including 1- and 2-inch equipment. Some 77.2% of all respondents reported having a studio available while 75.1% had editing equipment. Only 8.5% had the capacity to duplicate 10 or more tapes at one time.

Survey results indicate that 82.2% of all users have at least one camera; 36.3% have between one and three while 45.9% have more than three. Only 8.4% have more than 10 cameras. Studio cameras are owned by about 71% of respondents, portables by about 75%. About 78% have color cameras, 60% black-and-white.

How Video Is Used

In terms of actual video usage, employee training was the area cited most often by survey participants. About two thirds of all users—and more than 90% of the business/industry group—employ video for this purpose. Other important uses are student instruction, in-service education and public relations. Not surprisingly, among educational institutions the most frequent use is student instruction, with more than 80% of respondents checking this category. Table 3.3 presents a breakdown of responses on video use by each segment.

Personnel

Just under 90% of all users employ a video staff, with 87.1% employing a full-time staff. More than half of these consist of between one and three persons, whereas only 9.5% of respondents have more than 10 employees on the full-time video staff. Just over half of all respondents employ a part-time staff, with just over 25% employing one or two persons on a part-time basis. Less than a third of all users reported hiring additional personnel on an as-needed basis, and, not surprisingly, a majority (51.7%) do not employ a professional video engineer.

Only sketchy information was received on personnel budgets, with 44.6% of respondents unable or unwilling to provide figures. Among users who did respond, $25,000-$49,999 was the budget range most frequently mentioned. Only 10.1% of all respondents indicated personnel budgets of $100,000 or more.

In an attempt to identify the corporate or administrative department most frequently responsible for video production, users were asked to indicate the department to which the video facility reports. As Table 3.4 shows, 25% of all respondents specified the media or audiovisual depart-

Table 3.3: Uses of Video

Use	Percentage of Users					
	All Users (N=852)¹	Business/Industry (N=345)	Education (N=323)	Government (N=73)	Medical (N=67)	Nonprofit (N=31)
Employee training	66.2%	91.3%	44.0%	80.8%	46.3%	38.7%
Orientation	62.1	74.2	55.7	64.4	47.8	32.3
Student instruction	59.3	41.4	83.3	60.3	49.3	38.7
In-service education	56.7	47.2	67.2	65.8	55.2	41.9
Public relations	54.5	56.5	55.7	60.3	41.8	45.2
Continuing education	49.1	35.7	63.2	47.9	55.2	48.4
Management information	43.5	70.4	19.5	52.1	20.9	29.0
Documentation	42.6	45.5	43.7	46.6	31.3	25.8
Safety instruction	40.0	56.8	22.9	57.5	29.9	19.4
News & information	38.7	42.9	40.2	35.6	19.4	35.5
Sales & marketing	29.7	61.2	8.4	5.6	3.0	22.6
Research	22.7	18.3	25.4	28.8	25.4	19.4
Entertainment	19.1	10.7	30.7	12.3	19.4	16.1
Shareholder information	7.0	14.2	1.9	2.7	1.5	3.2
Other	5.4	2.3	8.7	2.7	9.0	6.5
Don't know/no answer	8.7	2.0	6.5	5.5	35.8	32.3

¹Includes 13 unclassified respondents.

Table 3.4: Department Supervising Video Facility

Department	Percentage of Users					
	All Users (N=852)	Business/Industry (N=345)	Education (N=323)	Government (N=73)	Medical (N=67)	Nonprofit (N=31)
Media or A/V	25.0%	9.9%	44.6%	15.1%	25.4%	12.9%
Training	14.0	24.3	2.5	30.1	4.5	3.2
Communications	12.3	15.1	13.6	2.7	4.5	12.9
Education	11.0	5.8	12.1	31.5	10.4	16.1
Personnel/human resources	8.2	15.7	0.6	9.6	3.0	16.1
Public relations	6.9	14.8	0.6	4.1	4.5	—
Marketing	4.2	10.1	0.3	—	—	—
Public affairs	2.5	4.1	0.6	4.1	—	3.2
Sales promotion	1.4	2.3	0.6	2.7	—	—
Other	13.4	6.7	24.8	—	10.4	9.7
No answer	11.0	4.3	8.7	8.2	40.3	32.3

Table 3.5: Production of Video Programming in 1979

Number of Programs Produced	All Users (N=1087)	Business/Industry (N=463)	Education (N=393)	Percentage of Users Government (N=92)	Medical (N=81)	Nonprofit (N=44)
0	7.3%	7.3%	6.1%	12.0%	2.5%	15.9%
1-5	16.3	16.6	12.7	26.1	22.2	13.6
6-12	21.4	23.1	19.8	20.7	21.0	18.2
13-24	15.2	16.2	15.3	15.2	14.8	11.4
25-59	23.7	24.2	24.9	12.0	28.4	22.7
60-99	5.5	6.7	4.8	6.5	3.7	2.3
100 or more	10.5	5.8	16.8	7.6	7.4	15.9

ment, while 12.3% mentioned communications and 14% training. Among business users, the training department had the highest percentage—nearly 25%, with personnel/human resources second at 15.7%. It might be assumed, in view of the high percentage of respondents indicating that employee training was the major use, that there is a close link between the personnel and the training departments and that in some firms they may be one and the same.

Programming

Nearly 93% of all users indicated that they had produced video programming during 1979. The majority specified between one and 24 programs, and only 16% overall said they had produced 60 or more. As Table 3.5 shows, education users were more likely to have produced a greater number of programs while government users produced relatively fewer.

Less than half of all users reported purchasing programs in 1979 and, of those who did, the majority had purchased between one and five programs. (See Table 3.6.) Even fewer respondents indicated that they had rented programs: more than two thirds said they had not rented any programs at all and, again, of those who did, the majority rented between one and five.

Table 3.6: Production/Purchase/Rental of Video Programming in 1979

Total Programs	Percentage of Users (N=1087)		
	Produced	Purchased	Rented
0	7.3%	57.1%	68.4%
1-5	16.3	21.3	14.7
6-12	21.4	10.5	6.6
13-24	15.2	4.2	3.5
25-59	23.7	3.7	3.7
60 or more	16.0	3.4	3.1

Looking toward the future, 64.3% expected production to increase during the next year. But respondents were less optimistic about future purchases and rentals with only 24.8% anticipating an increase in purchases and 19.8% expecting an increase in rentals. (See Table 3.7.)

Table 3.7: Organizations Expecting an Increase in Production/Acquisition of Programming in 1980

Anticipate Increase in:	All Users (N=1087)	Business/Industry (N=463)	Education (N=393)	Government (N=92)	Medical (N=81)	Nonprofit (N=44)
			Percentage of Users			
Production	64.3%	67.0%	60.8%	59.8%	70.4%	59.1%
Purchases	24.8	25.5	25.7	15.2	32.1	18.2
Rentals	19.8	16.6	25.7	15.2	19.8	11.4

The overwhelming majority of respondents took full responsibility for production with only 28.8% indicating that they had sought outside help.

As for production costs, nearly 20% of all users said they typically spent in excess of $2000 per program, although almost 10% said their typical costs were very low — $100 or less. Table 3.8 presents the respondents' replies to a question about typical, minimum and maximum production costs. It should be noted that a high percentage of users did not respond to this question. It is likely that many of those who did respond failed to include personnel and overhead costs in production costs, thus understating the figures.

Table 3.8: Cost of Producing a Video Program

| Amount | Percentage of Users (N=852) | | |
	Typical Expenditure	Minimum	Maximum
Under $100	9.7%	17.0%	1.8%
$100-199	5.2	6.9	2.7
$200-299	3.4	3.5	2.2
$300-599	9.0	8.0	4.9
$600-999	4.1	2.5	2.2
$1000-1999	8.5	4.6	5.5
$2000 plus	19.2	6.3	28.1
Don't know/no answer	41.0	51.2	52.6

Hardware Value and Purchasing Plans

Asked to set a value on the video hardware on hand, 36.7% of all respondents estimated that it was worth less than $100,000. Less than 15% valued their equipment at more than $500,000. (See Table 3.9.) Of those anticipating hardware purchases, more than half plan to spend less than $50,000. (See Table 3.10.) Among those who did plan purchases, the needs most frequently cited were for VTRs (45.7%) and cameras (40.2%) as shown in Table 3.11.

Budgets in general were moderate in size with 30.5% of all users indicating that less than $100,000 was allocated to the video effort. (See

Table 3.9: Value of Video Hardware on Hand

Value	All Users (N=852)	Business/Industry (N=345)	Percentage of Users Education (N=323)	Government (N=73)	Medical (N=67)	Nonprofit (N=31)
Under $100,000	36.7%	44.1%	32.2%	31.5%	29.9%	41.9%
$100,000 or more	43.9	42.3	52.0	43.8	28.4	19.4
$500,000 or more	13.0	11.6	16.4	11.0	7.5	—
Don't know/no answer	19.4	13.6	15.8	24.7	41.8	38.7

Table 3.10: New Equipment Budget for 1980

Amount	All Users (N=852)	Business/Industry (N=345)	Percentage of Users Education (N=323)	Government (N=73)	Medical (N=67)	Nonprofit (N=31)
Under $50,000	51.6%	47.2%	61.0%	49.3%	41.8%	48.4%
$50,000 or more	18.7	25.8	15.5	13.7	9.0	3.2
Don't know/no answer	29.7	27.0	23.5	37.0	49.3	48.4

Table 3.11: Anticipated Purchases in 1980

Equipment	Percentage of Users (N=852)		
	Yes, No $ Given	Less than $10,000	$10,000 or more
Cameras	13.6%	10.9%	15.7%
VTRs	16.9	15.5	13.2
Editing equipment	10.8	6.6	10.1
Audio equipment	12.9	14.0	4.0
Other production equipment:			
TV/monitor	0.7	1.6	1.2
Character generator	1.8	1.2	1.1
Time base corrector	1.3	0.5	2.0
Switchers	1.3	1.1	2.0
Special effects generator	0.4	0.4	0.1

Table 3.12.) However, the failure of 50% of respondents to reply to this question may mean that budgets are higher than survey results indicated. It should also be noted that budgets as high as $1 million-$2 million or more were reported by a small number of respondents.

As for the future, the video outlook is relatively optimistic. As shown in Table 3.13, more than 36% of all users said their budgets for 1979 were larger than last year's, and 34% expected to see an increase in 1980. However, 7.2% said the 1979 budget represented a decrease from the previous year, and 6.3% anticipated a decline in 1980. Five-year projections are difficult to make, since 46.7% did not respond to this question. However, 43.9% did predict an increase, and it is likely that more of the nonreporting group will see an increase than will record a decrease or remain the same.

SUMMARY

The majority of respondents to the *Video Register* survey reported having between one and 25 playback locations, with only 11% reporting more than 100. Nearly 90% employ a full-time video staff, and about 50% employ part-timers. Among all users, the media or A/V department was most likely to supervise video activity; among business users, the training department ranked first.

Table 3.12: Total Current Video Budget

Amount	Percentage of Users					
	All Users (N=852)	Business/Industry (N=345)	Education (N=323)	Government (N=73)	Medical (N=67)	Nonprofit (N=31)
Under $100,000	30.5%	27.8%	34.7%	35.6%	28.4%	19.4%
$100,000 or more	19.5	24.3	16.7	13.7	16.4	19.4
Don't know/no answer	50.0	47.8	48.6	50.7	55.2	61.3

Table 3.13: Comparison of Video Budgets, 1978, 1979, 1981-85

Respondents Anticipating:	Percentage of Users (N=852)		
	1979 Compared to 1978	1980 Compared to 1979	1981-85 Compared to 1980
Increase	36.5%	34.0%	43.9%
Decrease	7.2	6.3	2.9
Same	19.4	17.4	6.5
Don't know/ no answer	37.0	42.3	46.7

Employee training and orientation are the leading applications of video among survey respondents, followed closely by student instruction. In-service education, public relations and continuing education are other areas cited by a high percentage of users.

More than 90% of all respondents produced some programming in 1979, and about 65% expected production to increase in 1980. A much lower percentage reported purchase or rental of prepackaged programming, and even fewer expected such acquisitions to increase.

Hardware on hand was valued at less than $100,000 by 37% of respondents; more than half of users expected to spend under $50,000 for new equipment in 1980. Overall budget information is difficult to assess, since many users did not report this data. About 30% indicated modest video budgets—less than $100,000. Budget increases in 1980 were predicted by 34%, and 44% expected budgets to increase over a five-year period.

4

Business and Industry

The use of video by business and industry has grown steadily over the past decade. Although the rate of growth is difficult to quantify, there is no doubt that video is being used to achieve an increasingly broad range of corporate objectives, from employee training to morale boosting.

In addition, the composition of the business and industry market for nonbroadcast video appears to be changing. In the past, this market consisted primarily of large users with multiple branch offices, plants or factories scattered throughout the country, if not the world. By the start of the 1980s, relatively smaller companies were discovering that video could be an effective—and affordable—part of their operations.

There is a tremendous variety of programming produced by and for business/industry users, reflecting the great diversity among individual companies and the jobs within them. Most programming falls into one of two broad categories: employee training and corporate communications. Each of these encompasses a wide range of applications. In addition, there is a growth in video aimed at audiences outside the company; these applications include point-of-purchase displays in retail stores and public relations programming. The programs and case studies described in this chapter illustrate some of these uses of video.

GROWTH OF CORPORATE TELEVISION

The first Brush report on the nonbroadcast television market (see Chapter 2) concluded that more than 300 business and industrial firms were involved in video program production and distribution in 1973. The Brushes identified 75 private television networks, which they defined as systems with six or more locations. These included the Ford Video Network linking 5000 dealerships, the IBM network with 1000 playback locations in 40 countries, and a number of networks with more than 100 players operated by such companies as Xerox, Pepsi Cola, Burroughs, Merrill Lynch and others. In their second study three years later, the Brushes estimated that the size of the market had doubled since 1973, and that there were at least 200 networks with more than 20 locations.

Based on the 1979 *Video Register* survey, it is clear that the business/industry market for video has expanded tremendously since the Brushes' second report. (See summary of survey findings, later in this chapter.)

The ITVA

Another indication of this expansion is the growth of the International Television Association (ITVA), an organization for nonbroadcast video professionals whose membership is drawn primarily from corporate users. The association has only been in existence since 1973, when it was formed as the International Industrial Television Association by a merger between the Industrial Television Society (ITS) and the National Industrial Television Association (NITA). Both of these groups had been founded in the late 1960s to help the new professionals who were trying to meet business needs with a new medium—television. While the NITA, for example, had about 160 members in 1971, the ITVA numbered about 2300 by early 1980.

As the ITVA membership has been swelling, its composition has been changing as well. In the early years, the majority of the members were corporate training directors; the others were communications professionals and some broadcast and ETV professionals who had been hired to run the new video operations in corporations. Many of the earliest members came from the insurance and communications industries, from such firms as Prudential, Equitable Life, IBM and AT&T.

Membership in 1980 includes about 15% from educational and government institutions—in 1973 the "Industrial" was dropped from the title to reflect the growing number of members from other segments. The organization is still, however, geared primarily to business users. Training directors constitute about 50% of the membership while the other half could be called "media managers," working in such departments as public relations, communications, personnel, etc. A wide variety of industries are represented, among them accounting, transportation, retailing and manufacturing. As the ITVA has become more visible, offering its own programs, conferences, newsletter, etc., it has made business and industry more aware of the benefits of video.

ADVANTAGES OF VIDEO

Consistency and Flexibility

Video has multiple advantages as a training aid. First, video permits a high degree of consistency. All employees holding the same jobs and in need of the same training can see the same program, with the same degree of emphasis given to the most important points. Video also affords a high degree of flexibility — the time and place for the training session can easily be altered for the convenience of the employee and the manager or supervisor overseeing the training. This can be particularly important in sales training — personnel can view tapes introducing new products or explaining a new sales campaign individually at their convenience. The same advantages of consistency and flexibility apply in other areas — communicating new policies and directives, company financial news, or management changes, for example.

Cost-Effectiveness

Video can be a particularly cost-effective means of training and communication by eliminating the need for travel to and from regional or national conferences and, in some cases, even eliminating the need for such meetings altogether. Clearly, presenting a new product line or a change in corporate policy by means of video tape can be far cheaper than holding a conference with all the attendant expenses plus the costs of travel and time lost from normal activities.

This time (and, therefore, money) advantage is present even when no travel considerations are involved. A manager who must give frequent training sessions for new employees, for example, can tape the basic presentation and save the time he would have spent on multiple sessions.

Visual Impact

The visual impact of a dramatization or demonstration on video is another advantage of the medium. Video holds the viewer's attention more effectively than do print materials coupled with lectures or demonstrations. The effectiveness of printed materials depends on how conscientiously they are read, and, as one insurance company video manager put it, "people don't like to read any more." Even those who do "like to read" respond to the immediacy and visual appeal of a well-produced television program. In addition, there is the human quality of video. While an in-person presentation might be most effective in some situations, a video program can prove an excellent substitute by offering a "face-to-face" impression.

USING VIDEO FOR EMPLOYEE TRAINING

Video training programs include such applications as sales training, technical skills training, safety instruction, employee orientation and management development.

Sales Training

As early as the mid-1960s, business and industry recognized television's potential as a means of both training and motivating sales personnel scattered throughout the country. Video had two major advantages as a training medium: (1) it easily overcame the distribution problems inherent in the geographical distances between branch and regional offices, and (2) it could illustrate visually, as print material could not, effective sales techniques and explain clearly new products or changes to existing ones. An added advantage was that video programs could be viewed at the convenience of the salespeople.

One major video user in the insurance industry is the Prudential Insurance Co., which has a nationwide network of 850 video locations. (See case study.) Like most insurance companies, Prudential relies heavily on dramatizations in its sales training materials to demonstrate the most effective techniques for making contact with potential customers, describing the policies available and answering questions. Another insurance company, Mutual Benefit Life, uses similar programming. One of its tapes, "The Approach," shows a fictional agent approaching prospective clients while a narrator, in a voice-over, analyzes for the viewers how the most important selling points in the presentation are made.

Penn Mutual Life tapes role-playing sessions to show agents that personal habits or mannerisms may detract from their sales presentations. Agents can learn, for instance, to maintain eye contact with customers and to sit up straight during their presentations. The same basic dramatization/interview format is used by many other companies. The Pepsi Cola Company, for instance, has produced three major training series; one tape on merchandising and display includes an instant-replay segment in which the narrator reviews a salesperson's performance and points out the mistakes. U.S. Gypsum Company produced as a sales training tape a dramatization entitled "The Perfect Frame-Up," starring Humphrey Bogart and Mary Astor look-alikes, in which "Bogey" teaches his friend Max how to construct a door "fit for a princess and straight as the Holland Tunnel." In the end, Max gets the girl and Bogey delivers the moral: "When panels fit, you always get the perfect frame-up."

Skills Training

Dramatizations as well as videotaped lectures, voice-over demonstrations and straightforward demonstrations are used for skills training as well as sales training. At the Bendix Corp.'s Kansas City division, short video segments explain a variety of tasks ranging from filling out forms to soldering techniques. Hewlett-Packard uses videotaped dramatizations to train clerical workers in how to use the telephone. Illinois Bell Telephone has produced programs on how to handle irate customers and the importance of courtesy in dealing with the public.

Management Training

A number of companies use video in their management training programs. Gulf Oil of Canada, for example, has produced a series of management training programs to help new supervisors develop work-related skills. The course, "Management One," is divided into 30 modules and utilizes, in addition to video tapes, a mix of collateral materials and tests. Trainees proceed at their own pace and study only the skills they do not already have.

Playbacks of taped role-playing sessions are widely used in management training programs to analyze techniques and demonstrate errors. This application is particularly effective for interview training, performance appraisals and group dynamics training.

Related Applications

Closely related to training are programs designed to instruct employees in on-the-job safety; for the introduction and explanation of new products, methods or equipment; and for orientation of new employees and explanation of job benefit plans.

The International Paper Co. has produced an orientation package entitled "Corporate Overview" which introduces the company and describes its locations, organization, products and marketing. Owens-Corning has an employee orientation package of six 10-to-12-minute programs using voice-over and location footage to describe the company, its organization, and customer uses of its products. Employees also view tapes explaining benefit programs at Owens-Corning.

At Phillips Petroleum an animated character named "Phillip Allwell" was created to explain four employee benefit packages. Representatives of the company's benefits department answer Phillip's questions about the plans. One segment, taped on location at a hospital, illustrates aspects of the company health plan and includes interviews with employees who have received benefits.

USING VIDEO FOR CORPORATE COMMUNICATIONS

Corporate communications is an umbrella term covering a number of video applications: state-of-the-company reports, new management trends, changes in policy and long-range corporate plans, and employee recognition, among others.

Informational Programming

Examples of this type of programming were produced by Allis-Chalmers Corp., a major manufacturer of heavy equipment. Using the format of a press conference, one program entitled "Joint Venture Announcement" described an impending company reorganization plan and explained its effect on employees in the 10 divisions involved. A panel discussion format was used in another Allis-Chalmers production, a tape explaining expansion plans to employees in its Medium Motors Division near Cincinnati.

Fisher Scientific Co., a manufacturer and distributor of laboratory equipment, instruments and chemicals, distributes a 15-minute manager's quarterly report to employees. The first five minutes are devoted to a financial report and update on the current business climate. The rest is a mini-documentary "featurette" highlighting a particular Fisher division or company-related event.

A number of large corporations produce regular employee communications programs. GEICO uses a panel-discussion format modeled after "Meet the Press," featuring the chairman of the board and several employees discussing such topics as a new job evaluation program and the role of employees in current business plans. Pacific Telephone (see case study) produces a quarterly program designed for second-level management, utilizing a question-and-answer format with the company's chairman or president responding to questions.

Employee Morale

A number of companies are using video as a tool for raising employee morale. The Bendix Corp. has produced a number of short programs focusing on specific jobs within the company to give recognition to employees. Pacific Telephone produces a 15-minute biweekly program called "On Line," designed to involve nonmanagement employees more actively in company affairs and to boost their morale by acknowledging the roles they play.

In a related application, American Motors Corp. (Kenosha Division) has produced a number of programs designed specifically for the entertainment of employees on lunch and coffee breaks. Subjects have included lady wrestlers, a special Olympics for the retarded, coverage of a school swim meet that featured interviews with employees' children, scouting events, tips on gardening, and performances of local musical groups. Some entertainment programming is acquired from outside sources; such tapes have included programs on hunting and fishing and excerpts from network television shows.

OTHER APPLICATIONS

Outside the two main categories of video applications in business and industry—training and corporate communications—are several others. Some of these are closely related to the communications uses already discussed, but are aimed at an audience other than company employees.

- Sales. Some business/industry users have found video an effective way to present products directly to their potential customers. Retailers have set up point-of-sale players to draw customers to a display of merchandise and to make a sales pitch without a salesperson. Video programs can also be used by a salesperson as an aid in a presentation. One of General Motors' planned uses of video disc systems, for example, is to present product information to customers at the dealerships.

- Marketing support. Programs on how to use machinery or office products, for example, can be used by market support personnel to train customers, or can even be used by customers on their own. This reduces the time and cost of training and eliminates some of the difficulties of scheduling training time.

- Public relations. This might include programming about the company or some specific company project designed to enhance the corporate image among customers or community groups. Some corporate users have also produced programs specifically as a public service.

- Recruiting. Corporate personnel departments can present their companies in a dynamic way to potential employees. Video cassettes can be sent to colleges and universities, for example, to recruit students.

• Entertainment. One other use of video by some members of the business/industry segment is entertainment of customers, although users do not usually produce their own programs for this purpose. Some restaurants, for example, show cartoons and old movies for their patrons' entertainment. Several airlines are starting to replace film equipment on their aircraft with video equipment to entertain their passengers.

OFF-THE-SHELF PROGRAMS

The market for off-the-shelf video programming for use in business and industry has not developed at the same pace as has in-house production. (More than 50% of the users participating in the *Video Register* survey indicated that they had not purchased any prerecorded programming during the previous year and more than 70% indicated that they had not rented programming.)

Resistance to prerecorded materials in this market can be explained in part by competitive considerations and by the need for materials geared specifically to an individual company's operations. The use of video for sales training, skills training and, certainly, corporate communications relies on programming specifically designed to explain or illustrate a product or service the company views as unique.

The demand for off-the-shelf tapes is thus strongest in two areas where tailor-made programming is less important: management training and data processing. In addition, the market for motivational tapes is expanding.

A number of publishers produce and distribute video programming either specifically designed for use in business and industry or considered suitable for it although originally produced with some other market segment in mind. Among the largest are two Illinois-based firms which have concentrated on programming designed for instruction in data processing: Advanced Systems, Inc. (ASI) and Deltak, Inc.

ASI, a subdivision of URS Corp., has a video library with more than 2000 titles in data processing, management, engineering, manufacturing, marketing communications, security and safety, and personal development. Its materials include full-color video tapes, student guides, accompanying audio cassettes and coordinator guides. Its marketing is done on both a direct sales and subscription library basis. Subscribers may rent, on a monthly basis, any tape in the library. Costs range from about $40 per month to $120 per month, depending on the number of programs required.

Among ASI's most requested titles are "Data Processing Concepts," "Effective Interviewing," "ANS Cobol," "CICS/VS," the "Systems" series,

"How to Say No to a Rapist — and Survive," "Drucker on the Manager and the Organization" and the "Advanced Information Technology Curriculum," a series covering four subject areas — data communications, data networks, data bases and distributed data processing.

Deltak, a subsidiary of Prentice-Hall, also has a library of more than 2000 courses. Its most sought-after video training programs are designed for data processing instruction. They include "Distributive Data Processing," "Telecommunications," "Networking," "Data Bases," "Computer Security," "Reliability and Performance," "Office of the Future Technologies," "MRP Training for Manufacturing Organizations," "Energy Level Program Training," "Comprehensive Computer Operations Training for IBM Systems" and "Structural Information Systems Development Disciplines." Deltak develops its own programs on the basis of market research and also distributes programming acquired from other sources. It has sales offices in 20 cities in the United States and in 1980 formed a London subsidiary, Deltak, Ltd., which will operate in 15 countries.

In addition to these large, pioneering video publishers, a number of established publishers sell or lease video programming in the business and industrial market. They include BFA Educational Media, a division of CBS; BNA Communications, Inc., a division of the Bureau of National Affairs, Inc.; Edutronics, a McGraw Hill company; IDT (In-House Development and Training), a division of the American Management Association; Nightingale Conant Corp., a producer of motivational and sales training tapes; and Roundtable Films.

Most off-the-shelf programming designed for the business and industry market is available in all video formats as well as 16mm and 8mm film. Lengths vary depending on the subject matter. Much of what is currently available includes supplementary print materials, such as texts and workbooks. Those designed as part of or as a supplement to a formal instructional program often have accompanying teacher aids.

PROSPECTS

The prospects for growth within the business and industrial segment of the nonbroadcast market can be viewed from two perspectives. The first is the rapidity with which new users are adopting video as a communications and training tool. The second is the expanding number of uses of television among established users.

New Users

The current trend toward the use of video among small and medium-sized companies is a clear indication of its proven value. Corporate television has now been in existence for nearly three decades, and as its multiple applications become increasingly common in larger corporations, it has gained acceptance as a possibility for all companies. This trend has been helped by the fact that the price of a basic video system—a portable camera and a VTR— has dropped to the point where many companies can afford to experiment with television without making a major investment.

Even more important, as other costs such as travel expenses and salaries continue to rise, the relative cost of using video for specific applications has become even lower. Potential corporate users accustomed to a cost/benefit approach to management have been able to see that investment in video may not only save money, but may also increase effectiveness. These users are more likely to invest in new equipment; users in other segments, even if they apply a cost/benefit approach, may not have the resources at hand to implement such a decision.

Another element making video attractive to new users is that of competition and/or prestige. The more video is used in a certain field, the more likely it is that companies in the field will feel they have to use it. Cost factors aside, many executives are concerned that their companies be current or up-to-date in methods of management and communications. In addition, many may find it an appealing idea to be seen on television and possibly to be recorded for posterity. If their counterparts in the company down the road are already appearing on TV, all the more reason to opt for video.

Further, large corporations with many locations are actively courted by major video suppliers. A manufacturer can virtually create a market for its product if it can work out an agreement with a user with a very large network. In the early 1970s, for example, when Sony introduced its U-matic recorder, it contracted with the Ford Motor Company to deliver 5000 players at an early date. More recently, the General Motors Corp. became the first large user of the DiscoVision video disc system in 1979. Under this arrangement, more than 10,000 dealers in all five divisions of GM will be using the Universal-Pioneer machine to play programming on product, sales and service information. The fact that such a highly visible corporation is using the system should encourage acceptance and stimulate sales among other corporate users.

Identifying the smaller firms most likely to be new users of video is difficult — manufacturers who maintain direct contact only with their larger customers are simply not aware of who the small users are and what types of businesses they represent. Similarly, both dealers and producers are unable to assess types of new users.

Expanding Applications

In addition to moving to new technology, established users tend to find increasing numbers of applications for video in their organizations. Once a company has mastered and come to rely on basic types of training and communications programming, its executives are more likely to think of video as an alternative when new information, products, problems or projects come up.

One type of video programming that should become more widespread is that used for sales/marketing. This includes point-of-purchase display programs and those used by salespeople to present new products or information. The advantages of reduced costs and consistency of presentation apply particularly here, so this application should gain in acceptance in companies of all sizes.

Programs designed to raise employee morale — featuring interviews with employees, recognizing the importance of specific jobs, etc. — are also likely to proliferate. The fact that a number of companies produce news programs to keep employees up-to-date on internal and external matters affecting the business testifies to the increasing perception of the role of television as an effective means of improving relations between employees and management. The trend toward providing employees with entertainment programming appears to be accelerating, a development that lends credence to the idea that television may prove to be a highly cost-effective means of building employee good-will, and, as a result, increased productivity.

Programming produced for employee viewing may also lend itself to public relations and community relations efforts. Programming of local interest could be made available for viewing on cable television as a means of building good-will within a community. It would appear that eventually programming produced for use within business and industry could serve a much wider audience than it now does, thus greatly increasing both its impact and its cost-effectiveness.

It must be emphasized, however, that not every video application is suitable to every company. Any decision to use video must be weighed from a highly individual standpoint. The key questions to be answered before opting for video in any given situation are (1) Is there a definable need? and (2) Is video the most cost-effective way to meet this need?

The following section presents data from corporate users who have made a commitment to video services and who responded to the 1979 *Video Register* survey. It will be followed by case studies of six firms actively engaged in video application.

SURVEY FINDINGS

A total of 463 business/industry firms responded to the *Video Register* survey, representing 42.5% of the total sample. (Subgroups of this category, and their percentages of the total sample, were listed in Table 3.1.) This section of *Video in the '80s* summarizes the responses of the major business/industry groups: manufacturing/industrial, financial (including banks, insurance firms and other financial services) and service industries (including utilities, transportation, communications, retail/wholesale and other). Because insurance companies are among the oldest and largest corporate users of video, some data from this subgroup of the financial segment will be presented separately. Likewise, some separate data will be presented for a relatively new group of users, wholesale/retail establishments.

Size of Network

About 53% of all business/industry respondents reported networks of between one and 25 locations; nearly 16% had more than 100 locations. More insurance companies reported large networks than any other single group—some 24% indicating more than 100 locations. This group also reported more medium-sized (50-100 sites) networks than other users. Table 4.1 shows the size of video networks in all business/industry groups. (For additional data and comparison with all users, see Table 3.2.)

Uses of Video

The overwhelming majority of business/industry respondents used video for employee training, with this application leading all others in all groups. Orientation (often linked with training) and management information were other significant areas of video use in all groups. Sales and marketing ranked high among financial institutions, particularly insurance companies, while safety instruction was a major application in manufacturing/industrial firms. Table 4.2 provides a breakdown of video use as reported by each segment of the business/industry category. (For additional data and comparison with all users, see Table 3.3.)

Supervision of Video Services

The departments most likely to supervise business/industry video facilities were training and communications, with personnel/human resources also mentioned frequently. (As noted in Chapter 3, training and

Table 4.1: Size of Video Network

No. Playback Locations	All Business/ Industry (N=463)	Mfg./Industrial Firms (N=239)	Percentage of Users			
			All Financial (N=70)	Insurance (N=30)	All Services (N=154)	Wholesale/ Retail (N=46)
1-10	29.8%	29.7%	28.6%	21.6%	30.5%	32.6%
11-25	23.5	24.7	10.0	10.8	27.9	41.3
26-50	12.3	12.6	18.6	24.3	9.1	6.5
51-100	12.1	11.7	17.1	18.9	10.4	10.9
101-300	13.0	12.6	20.0	21.6	10.4	4.4
Over 300	2.8	2.5	2.9	2.7	3.2	2.2
Unspecified	1.1	0.4	1.4	—	1.9	—
No response	5.4	5.9	1.4	—	6.5	2.2

Table 4.2: Uses of Video

Use	Percentage of Users					
	All Business/Industry (N=345)	Mfg./Industrial Firms (N=174)	All Financial (N=64)	Insurance (N=35)	All Services (N=107)	Wholesale/Retail (N=28)
Employee training	91.3%	92.5%	90.6%	94.3%	89.7%	100.0%
Orientation	74.2	75.9	73.4	77.1	72.0	82.1
Mgmt. information	70.4	73.0	70.3	77.1	66.4	71.4
Sales & marketing	61.2	63.2	70.3	80.0	52.3	46.4
Safety instruction	56.8	68.4	28.1	37.1	55.1	53.6
Public relations	56.5	58.6	48.4	51.4	57.9	28.6
In-service education	47.2	50.0	46.9	48.6	43.0	25.0
Documentation	45.5	50.0	26.6	34.3	49.5	39.3
News & information	42.9	42.5	40.6	51.4	44.9	25.0
Student instruction	41.4	40.8	39.1	42.9	43.9	32.1
Continuing education	35.7	39.1	42.2	40.0	26.2	17.9
Research	18.3	23.6	10.9	11.4	14.0	3.6
Shareholder information	14.2	13.8	14.1	17.1	15.0	3.6
Entertainment	10.7	12.6	6.3	8.6	10.3	14.3
Other	2.3	1.7	3.1	—	2.8	7.1
Don't know/no answer	2.0	0.6	3.1	—	3.7	—

personnel are likely to be the same department in many companies.) A significant percentage of financial companies, including insurance firms, assigned jurisdiction over video services to the marketing department. Data on video supervision are summarized in Table 4.3. (For additional data and comparison with all users, see Table 3.4.)

1979 Program Production

Most (93%) of the business/industry users indicated that they had produced some video programs in 1979. (See Table 4.4.) The majority specified between 1 and 24 programs, and 12.5% reported 60 or more. Among the subsegments, the manufacturing/industrial respondents were slightly more likely to have produced some programming—95% had—but less likely to have produced 60 or more. The financial group tended to have produced a larger number of programs; this was especially true of the insurance users, 24% of whom said they had produced 60 or more programs in 1979. Although 10% of the service industry companies and 9% of the wholesale/retail users said they had produced 60 programs or more, 12% of the former and 13% of the latter group reported no programming in 1979. (For comparison with all users, see Table 3.5.)

1980 Programming

As Table 4.5 indicates, more than 60% of business/industry respondents anticipated an increase in video production in 1980. A far lower percentage planned to increase purchases of off-the-shelf programming, and still fewer anticipated a rise in rentals of such programming. (For comparison with all users, see Table 3.7.)

Hardware Expenditures

As shown in Table 4.6, about 44% of business/industry users valued their video hardware at under $100,000. In the wholesale/retail group, this relatively modest investment was characteristic of more than 70%, reflecting the fact that video is a rather new phenomenon among these users. Conversely, among the insurance firms, long-established video users, the majority set their hardware value at $100,000 or more, and 11% estimated $1 million or more. The subsegment of all service industries was second most likely to have hardware valued at $100,000 or more, with 48% so reporting. Overall, 12% of business/industry users said their video hardware was worth $500,000 or more. (For comparison with all users, see Table 3.9.)

Table 4.3: Department Supervising Video Facility

Department	Percentage of Users					
	All Business/ Industry (N=345)	Mfg./Industrial Firms (N=174)	All Financial (N=64)	Insurance (N=35)	All Services (N=107)	Wholesale/ Retail (N=28)
Training	24.3%	23.0%	17.2%	14.3%	30.8%	53.6%
Personnel/human resources	15.7	14.4	17.2	17.1	16.8	28.6
Communications	15.1	15.5	21.9	28.6	10.3	7.1
Public relations	14.8	13.2	9.4	11.4	20.6	—
Marketing	10.1	9.8	18.8	20.0	5.6	3.6
Media or A/V	9.9	10.9	3.1	2.9	12.1	3.6
Education	5.8	5.7	10.9	8.6	2.8	—
Public affairs	4.1	4.0	1.6	—	5.6	—
Sales promotion	2.3	1.7	1.6	2.9	3.7	7.1
Other	6.7	11.5	1.6	—	1.9	—
No answer	4.3	1.7	4.7	2.9	8.4	3.6

Table 4.4: Production of Video Programming in 1979

No. of Programs	Percentage of Users					
	All Business/ Industry (N=463)	Mfg./Industrial Firms (N=239)	All Financial (N=70)	Insurance (N=37)	All Services (N=154)	Wholesale/ Retail (N=46)
None/no reponse	7.3%	5.4%	4.3%	—	11.7%	13.0%
1-12	39.7	42.3	34.3	32.4	38.3	32.6
13-24	16.2	16.3	15.7	10.8	16.2	15.2
25-59	24.2	27.6	30.0	32.4	16.2	21.7
60-99	6.7	5.0	11.4	18.9	7.1	8.7
100 or more	5.8	3.3	4.3	5.4	10.4	8.7

Table 4.5: Organizations Expecting an Increase in Production/Acquisition of Programming in 1980

Anticipate Increase in:	Percentage of Users					
	All Business/ Industry (N=463)	Mfg./Industrial Firms (N=239)	All Financial (N=70)	Insurance (N=37)	All Services (N=154)	Wholesale/ Retail (N=46)
Production	67.0%	67.8%	65.7%	64.9%	66.2%	60.9%
Purchases	25.5	27.2	21.4	16.2	24.7	30.4
Rentals	16.6	16.7	12.9	13.5	18.2	19.6

Table 4.6: Value of Video Hardware on Hand

Value	All Business/ Industry (N=345)	Mfg./Industrial Firms (N=174)	Percentage of Users All Financial (N=64)	Insurance (N=35)	All Services (N=107)	Wholesale/ Retail (N=28)
Under $100,000	44.1%	46.6%	39.1%	34.3%	43.0%	71.4%
$100,000 or more	42.3	38.5	43.8	51.4	47.7	28.6
$500,000 or more	11.6	11.5	15.6	22.9	9.3	—
Don't know/no answer	13.6	14.9	17.2	14.3	9.3	—

Insurance users were also most likely to have larger budgets for new equipment purchases in the coming year. In this group, 29% said they planned to spend $50,000 or more on new hardware, compared to 26% for business/industry users as a whole. (Note that 27% of the business/ industry users did not respond to this question at all.) As indicated in Table 4.7, users in all groups in this segment were more likely to have new equipment budgets of less than $50,000; this was particularly true in the wholesale/retail group, where 68% of respondents reported a budget in that range. (For comparison with all users, see Table 3.10.)

Video Budgets

Table 4.8 compares total video budgets of the various business/industry groups. It shows that a higher percentage of insurance companies had high video budgets—$100,000 or more—and that wholesale/retail firms were most likely to have budgets under that amount. Here again, a large number of respondents were unable or unwilling to provide budget figures. It should also be noted that budgets of "$100,000 or more" went as high as $1 million or more for 2% of business/industry users. (For comparison with all users, see Table 3.12.)

Other Findings

Equipment and facilities

• The ¾-inch format was used by the highest percentage of business/ industry respondents. About 56% of the manufacturing firms, 73% of financial firms (including insurance companies) and 49% of service companies (including wholesale/retail) reported having ¾-inch equipment. About one third of the respondents had ½-inch VTRs; less than 6% reported other formats including 1- and 2-inch equipment.

• Nearly three quarters of the manufacturing and financial institutions and about 70% of the service firms maintained video studios; 84% of insurance companies alone and 65% of the wholesale/retail group had studios.

• Editing equipment was reported by about 75% of manufacturing firms, 77% of financial firms, 92% of insurance companies, 71% of service companies and 65% of wholesale/retail firms.

• At least 80% of users in all business segments had cameras; the great majority had between one and three. About 78% had color cameras, 45% black-and-white; 61% had studio cameras, 67% portables.

• Service industry firms reported the greatest capacity to duplicate 10 or

Table 4.7: New Equipment Budget for Coming Year

Amount	Percentage of Users					
	All Business/Industry (N=345)	Mfg./Industrial Firms (N=174)	All Financial (N=64)	Insurance (N=35)	All Services (N=107)	Wholesale/Retail (N=28)
Under $50,000	47.2%	47.7%	48.4%	45.7%	45.8%	67.8%
$50,000 or more	25.8	27.0	23.4	28.6	25.2	10.7
Don't know/no answer	27.0	25.3	28.1	25.7	29.0	21.4

Table 4.8: Total Current Video Budget

Amount	Percentage of Users					
	All Business/Industry (N=345)	Mfg./Industrial Firms (N=174)	All Financial (N=64)	Insurance (N=35)	All Services (N=107)	Wholesale/Retail (N=28)
Under $100,000	27.8%	28.7%	26.6%	22.9%	27.1%	42.9%
$100,000 or more	24.3	25.9	25.0	31.4	21.5	7.1
Don't know/no answer	47.8	45.4	48.4	45.7	51.4	50.0

more tapes at a time, with 16% indicating the ability to do so.

Personnel

• Full-time video staffs were employed by approximately 82% of manufacturing firms, 91% of financial institutions, 97% of insurance companies, 84% of service companies and 80% of wholesale/retail users. Part-time video personnel were much less common, with only 46% of manufacturing, 36% of financial and 40% of service firms reporting any, usually one or two.

• Video staffs of between one and six persons were employed by about 65% of manufacturing firms, 67% of financial companies, 59% of insurance companies, 54% of service industry firms and 61% of wholesale/retailers.

• Large video staffs (seven or more) were reported by a higher percentage of insurance companies than any other segment. These companies were also the least likely to employ part-time video personnel.

• Less than half of all business/industry respondents hired additional staff for special projects; the highest percentage of "yes" responses to this question came from financial firms (about 44%).

• Video engineers were on the staff of about 31% of manufacturing companies, 41% of financial firms, 46% of insurance companies, 43% of service industry organizations and only 24% of wholesale/retail companies.

• Although many of the business/industry users did not respond to the question on personnel budgets, the majority of those who did reported one in the range of $25,000 to $99,999.

Programming

• Off-the-shelf program purchases were reported by about 43% of manufacturers, 51% of financial organizations, 49% of insurance companies, 36% of service companies and 41% of wholesale/retail firms. Users most commonly purchased between one and five programs per year.

• Fewer than 30% of respondents in any segment reported rental of programming.

• About half of the manufacturing group contracted with outside companies for program production. Other segments were less likely to do so.

• With the exception of insurance companies, the cost of a "typical" video production was most often placed at $2000 or more. In the insurance group, a figure of $1000-$1999 was reported most often. (A high percentage of users did not supply information on production costs.)

Anticipated purchases

• Cameras. About 42% of the manufacturing firms said they were planning to purchase cameras in 1980, with 21% mentioning a budget of $10,000 or more. In the financial group, 38% of the respondents were planning camera purchases, 20% with a budget of $10,000 or more; among insurance users, 40% anticipated camera purchases, 26% with a budget of $10,000 or more. Among the service firms, 48% anticipated camera purchases and 20% reported a budget of $10,000 or more; in the wholesale/retail subsegment, 46% said they were planning to buy cameras and 11% mentioned a budget of $10,000 or more.

• VTRs. Purchase of VTRs was anticipated by 51% of the manufacturing firms, 42% of the financial firms, 37% of insurance users, 44% of the service industries respondents and 22% of the wholesale/retail companies. Budgets of $10,000 or more for VTR purchases were reported by 21% of the manufacturing group, 14% of all financial users, 14% of insurance firms, 16% of service firms overall and 4% of wholesale/retail firms.

• Editing equipment. Plans to purchase editing equipment were indicated by 31% of the manufacturing firms, 22% of financial firms, 17% of insurance companies, 34% of service industries users and 21% of wholesale/retail respondents. A budget of $10,000 or more was mentioned by 16% of the manufacturers, 17% of the financial firms, 6% of the insurance users, 14% of service companies and 4% of the wholesale/retail respondents.

• Lights. Planned purchase of lights in 1980 was reported by 21% of the manufacturing group, 19% of the financial firms, 17% of insurance companies, 21% of the service industries respondents and 21% of the wholesale/retail users. The financial group was most likely to have budgeted $10,000 or more for the purchase of lights.

• Audio equipment. Thirty-one percent of the manufacturers, 28% of the financial firms, 34% of insurance companies, 29% of the service group and 19% of wholesale/retail firms said they were planning to buy audio equipment in 1980.

• Other production equipment. Some of the anticipated purchases include a monitor, mentioned by 5% of the manufacturing firms and 5% of financial respondents; a character generator, reported by 5% each of manufacturers and financial firms; and a time base corrector, indicated by 3% of the manufacturers, 5% of the financial firms and 6% of the service industry respondents. In addition, 4% of the manufacturers, 5% of the financial firms and 2% of the service companies said they were planning to purchase switchers, and 3% of the financial firms said they were going to buy a special effects generator.

Anticipated budgets

• Budget increases in 1980 over 1979 were projected by about 50% of the manufacturing and financial companies, 49% of insurance firms, 38% of service companies and 46% of wholesale/retail users. (Many respondents did not answer this question.)
• Five-year budget increases were projected by about 62% of manufacturing firms, 56% of financial companies, 54% of insurance companies, 42% of service firms and 64% of wholesale/retail users. (Here again, a high percentage of users did not provide budget information.)

CASE STUDIES

BENDIX CORP., KANSAS CITY DIVISION
P.O. Box 1159
Kansas City, MO 64141

The Bendix Corp.'s Kansas City facility handles classified U.S. government contract work producing electronic, mechanical and plastic components for military weapons. It employs 6000 persons in an enormous facility and utilizes video primarily for employee news and information in a morale-building effort. It has been involved with video since 1976. A total of six ¾-inch VTRs are located throughout the plant in high-traffic areas and in sites set aside for employees awaiting security clearance before beginning their jobs.

The media services department produces three regularly scheduled programs for employees. One is a three-minute weekly news program, which is run continuously every day during lunch hours; another is a three-minute feature, presented weekly, on a human interst or technical subject. There is also a continuous display showing the weather, Bendix stock prices and other employee information. The main thrust of video activity is employee recognition. "People here are hungry for recognition," explains a media services specialist. "We try to include as much employee footage as possible."

Because of the highly technical nature of the work, relatively little television is used in employee training. One or two "how-to" tapes, focussing on the manufacturing process, are produced monthly. Each runs between five and 15 minutes in length. Most training programs are designed to explain nonclassified and nontechnical tasks such as filling out forms, soldering techniques and the use of static sensitive devices. One 15-minute program is produced each quarter to describe and explain some aspect of the firm's production and technology. A recent one was on the use of foam. Some programming is also produced for the community relations department.

Bendix has a studio equipped with two studio and one portable color camera, as well as editing equipment. It is staffed by two full-time employees. The department produced 124 programs during the past year and expects production to increase in the future. Occasionally, packaged programs are purchased or rented from outside sources.

The value of the video hardware is estimated at $60,000. There is no video budget. Instead, the media services department makes specific requests when funds are needed for equipment or supplies and allocations are determined by the director of the employee relations division. In fiscal 1979 approximately $10,000 was spent on production. There are no firm plans for new equipment purchases in 1980.

PACIFIC TELEPHONE CO.
116 New Montgomery St.
San Francisco, CA 94105

The Pacific Telephone Co. is a very large user of video. A total of 1000 locations are equipped with playback machines, and studio facilities are extensive.

Pacific Telephone traces its video effort back 10 years and attributes it to the encouragement by American Telephone and Telegraph Co. of Bell System companies to consider using television for corporate communications and training. Today, Pacific Telephone has regularly scheduled informational/motivational programming that reaches all of its 110,000 employees bi-weekly. It also relies heavily on video for management information, public relations, marketing, employee orientation and other personnel-related matters and for training.

The principal audience for Pacific Telephone's 15-minute, bi-weekly video program, "On Line," is nonmanagement employees and district supervisors. The show was designed to involve these employees more actively in company affairs and to boost morale by acknowledging and focusing on the roles they play. For management-level employees, the video department produces five or six live telecasts per year transmitted to 15 or 20 offices throughout the state. These provide a link between the chairman of the board and other senior officers and middle management executives. In addition, there is a quarterly program designed for second-level management with a question and answer format that features the chairman or the president responding to questions from the audience.

Other programming includes the taping of the remarks of the chairman of the board and the company president at the annual meeting of shareholders, addresses to company employees by political candidates during statewide campaigns, and a number of programs designed to update employee training and for orientation of new employees.

Pacific Telephone has two video production studios, one in San Francisco and another in Pasadena. Construction of a new San Francisco facility, originally scheduled for 1980, has been temporarily postponed by the company for financial reasons. The value of video equipment already on hand is estimated at $1.5 million. The video operating budget is $1.3 million, representing a 300% increase from 1978 to 1979. The 1980 budget is expected to be the same as 1979's, but over the next five years, the budget is expected to rise by 6% to 10%.

There is a staff of 14 full-time employees, and additional staffers and/or contractors are hired for specific productions. Each studio has a professional video engineer. At present, Pacific Telephone produces approximately 100 programs per year. No programming is purchased or rented from outside sources.

J.C. PENNEY CO.
1301 Avenue of the Americas
New York, NY 10019

J.C. Penney Co. began producing television programming in 1976 in order to communicate to its retail outlets a change in its approach to women's fashion. Initially, this new means of communicating with the stores was tested in 25 locations, but by 1979 this network had grown to 550 units. In 1980 another 125 locations will be added.

Television programming is produced strictly for internal use to convey new corporate directions to the field, to introduce or describe products and to explain company-wide policies on such subjects as energy management. One recent program introduced a new microwave oven to be sold in the stores; another explained what was "revolutionary" about a new type of pantyhose being introduced.

A highly successful video effort used programming to subsititute for live presentations at seasonal merchandise meetings. The tape, featuring Christmas toys, was distributed directly to all stores in an attempt to cut the costs and travel time involved in holding regional meetings. The tape included footage of the television commercials being used to advertise the toys and was accompanied by print materials to supplement the information. The program was considered so effective that similar productions will be used to substitute for other merchandise meetings.

Penney's in-house programming also includes some educational productions for new employees and some for employee communication — for example, a tape was distributed in connection with a recent United Fund campaign. Although no off-the-shelf programs are purchased by the audiovisual department for training purposes, some tapes have been acquired by other departments for use in management development and data processing training. Unlike other retailing companies, Penney's has not adopted video for point-of-purchase sale use on the theory that "people come to the stores to shop, not to watch television."

Reflecting the company's growing commitment to video, a new studio twice the size of the current facility is under construction and should be completed and in production in 1980. At present, an estimated $1.5 million in television hardware, including four color cameras and editing equipment, is in use. A total of $800,000 has been budgeted for new equipment purchases in 1980 — half of that will be used for the 125 new VTRs to be placed in the field. The remainder will be used for production equipment including off-line editing equipment and, possibly, a second ENG camera. Penney's operating video budget is $700,000, a figure that includes staff salaries. There are 32 employees in the audiovisual department. Seven of these (including a professional television engineer) work only on video production. There is a creative staff of 18, but the number associated with television programming varies as this staff also has responsibility for other audiovisual and some print materials.

In 1979 the company produced a total of 52 programs, and it expects to maintain this level of production through 1980. The costs per program can range from $2000 to $15,000. The staff aims for high technical quality in the belief that viewers are accustomed to broadcast quality television and that "anything less could have a negative effect."

THE PRUDENTIAL INSURANCE CO.
Prudential Plaza
Newark, NJ 07101

The Prudential Insurance Co. employs 62,000 people at 850 locations throughout the United States and abroad. Each of its 850 offices is equipped with ¾-inch video playback equipment used in conjunction with sales training, marketing, management communication and employee orientation programming.

Prudential has had a video production facility since 1966, when its audiovisual department first installed a pilot system following the lead of the Equitable Life Insurance Co. The system was enlarged in 1967, and in 1970 a proposal was made to replace the existing A/V facility with video. It took four years before approval was forthcoming for a test of video in sales skills training. The test was so successful that Prudential approved installation of its network of 850 VTRs in 1977.

Today, the primary use of video is in sales training for agents in 700 field offices, for management training at the home office and for home office training designed to provide general information about insurance for staff level supervisors and clerical personnel. Most of the sales training materials illustrating basic skills run between 35 and 40 minutes in length; there are also some 10-minute programs that are largely motivational and inspirational in nature.

As a rule, video is not used in marketing to customers but as part of sales promotional programs to introduce new products to the field or to familiarize agents with a new sales or advertising campaign. However, Prudential has produced a few customer programs as part of its efforts to sell large group plans.

In the management information area, programming is designed to teach such skills as interviewing techniques for use in a number of different situations ranging from hiring and firing to performance evaluations. Most of these programs are 40 minutes long and are used in conjunction with other training materials and workshops. The company also has produced a number of programs to explain employee benefit plans.

During 1979, Prudential produced 40 programs, purchased eight from outside sources and rented four others. The A/V department, which remains responsible for video production at the corporate level, has a four-camera studio with electronic editing equipment and a staff of eight full-time employees (including a video engineer) and four part-time workers. It places the value of its equipment at $500,000 and budgeted $75,000 for new equipment purchases in 1979. This amount includes $10,000 for VTRs, $20,000 for editing equipment, $18,000 for "miscellaneous electronics," $2,000 for lights and $25,000 for audio equipment.

The company estimates that it spends about $30,000 per production (including the cost of duplication). The total video budget is estimated at $1.8 million, including equipment purchases but excluding salaries. The video budget has been increasing steadily, up 6% to 10% in 1979; it should rise between 1% and 5% in 1980. An increase of between 1% and 5% over the next five years is anticipated.

SEDCO INC.
1905 N. Akard
Dallas, TX 75201

Sedco contracts rigs and crews to oil companies for use in offshore drilling. It has a number of subsidiaries, including companies engaged in the design and construction of equipment for oil exploration and drilling. The video department based at the parent company's headquarters in Dallas provides training materials for between 4000 and 5000 employees located on 32 offshore drilling vessels and more than 20 land-based oil drilling rigs.

Sedco first explored the use of video for training purposes in 1972, but was dissatisfied with the state-of-the-art of the equipment then available and shelved its plans. In 1975 it began to install ¾-inch video tape players to replace the 16mm film equipment used on rigs for employee entertainment (the offshore rigs had no other access to entertainment and employees remain on the rigs for weeks at a time without returning to land). That same year Sedco sent Jerry Hodges, its newly-hired video manager, to Iran to discuss recurrent problems with drill pipe equipment. The failure rate with the equipment was high — pipes were wearing out at the rate of one every six months, at an annual replacement cost of about $27 million. Hodges took a Sony color camera and a portable video tape recorder with him and met in Iran with an authority on drill pipes. Together, they devised a five-part video series entitled "Care and Handling of Drill Pipes." The cost of production was $2000; within a year, use of the tapes had increased the life of drill pipes 100%, thus saving Sedco the entire replacement cost. The success of the series resulted in a move toward video training.

Today, Sedco's five-person video staff produces 20 video training programs per year at a cost of $1500 each, exclusive of travel, equipment amortization and salaries. The company has no studio and does all production work in the field. Post-production is done outside, although Sedco does have in-house capacity to duplicate 75 copies. It also has three color cameras, a ¾-inch editing system and a network of more than 120 ½-inch VTRs on offshore and land rigs as well as in its Dallas corporate headquarters.

Among Sedco's video training programs are a 20-part series on the maintenance and repair of the diesel electric generators used to supply the offshore rigs with power, as well as series on blowout preventions, mud pump maintenance, sub sea connectors and drilling lines — all involving highly specialized types of equipment. In addition to producing its own programs, Sedco purchases programming when it can secure duplicating rights for less than the $1500 it would spend on its own productions. It does not rent programming.

The video manager reports directly to the corporate vice president for personnel. There is no annual equipment budget — requests are made on an "as needed" basis. The value of equipment on hand in mid-1980 was estimated at $125,000. The video department expect to replace its editing system and to propose purchase of an Ampex VPR 1-inch recorder, additional monitors and an additional Sony ¾-inch recorder.

Although the bulk of Sedco's programming is used for employee training, the video department has produced some tapes for other applications. In 1979, for example, it produced a 2½-hour sales presentation in three weeks, at a cost of $45,000 (including the cost of translation into Chinese). The cost of having an equivalent program produced outside was estimated at $150,000. Other nontraining uses have included documentation of new equipment for insurance purposes and for company history and an occasional program designed for corporate communications. The video division also continues to arrange for entertainment programs distributed to the offshore rigs.

No specific plans have been formulated to expand video activities, although the video department does expect to begin producing tapes for more company divisions eventually. The department's current inclination is to remain small on the theory that the larger it grows the more it will have to sacrifice in efficiency and cost-effectiveness.

UNION CARBIDE
270 Park Ave.
New York, NY 10017

Union Carbide is one of the 25 largest industrial companies in the United States. It has 113,371 employees working in five industry segments: chemicals and plastics, gases and related products, metals and carbons, batteries and home and automotive products, and specialty products. From its New York City headquarters it supplies 350 locations around the world with video materials for training, management communication and employee communication.

Training represents the largest focus of Union Carbide's video activities.

The company has produced training tapes for metals, chemicals, plastics, management development, medical and labor relations personnel. It produced 14 programs on purchasing techniques for the corporate purchasing division and a program on how to operate new heating, ventilation and air conditioning systems in its corporate headquarters. Tapes average 15 minutes in length.

One example of management communication through video was the production of a taped report from Union Carbide's president on the future of the company though 1983 for distribution to top corporate management and to field management. Employee communication productions have included the highlights of the annual meeting of shareholders, a program on physical fitness and several programs designed to explain various company benefits. Approximately 5% of the video productions are for external use in community relations activities and sales promotions for exhibit at trade shows.

Union Carbide does not maintain a studio at its New York headquarters, but shoots all tapes on location. It has nine full-time employees on the staff of the corporate audiovisual communications department, including a professional video engineer. Additional staff is hired for specific productions and the company does contract with outside service companies as needed for editing work on its productions. During 1979, some 50 video programs were produced. No prerecorded programs were purchased or rented from outside sources.

Union Carbide values its video equipment at $150,000 and planned to spend an additional $125,000 in 1979 on cameras, VTRs and editing equipment. It estimates that it spends an average of $6500 per production from a total video budget of $350,000. The cost of each program is charged back to client departments within the company which call on the A/V unit for program production as needed.

In addition to the video unit at the corporate level there are four other units within Union Carbide that produce programming. More than 20 persons are assigned to these other video units.

Increasing amounts have been allocated to the corporate video unit during the past year — the budget increased by more than 16% in 1979 and should increase again by between 11% and 15% in 1980. The next five years are expected to bring additional increases in staff, hardware and programming, but no specific figures are available as yet.

5

Education

The use of television in education dates back to the 1950s, when colleges and universities adopted closed circuit television systems to accommodate large classes by placing students in classrooms scattered throughout the campus rather than in one large lecture hall. Government grants in the 1960s encouraged school systems to acquire video equipment and programming at the elementary and secondary levels. Early enthusiasm for video in schools has diminished somewhat as a result of budgetary restrictions, resistance on the part of teachers, and a trend of "back to basics" in instructional materials — in other words to textbooks. However, the existing market for video is large, particularly at the higher levels.

NATURE OF THE MARKET

The El-Hi Market

The extent of television use in schools was measured in 1976 in a joint study by the National Center for Education Statistics (NCES) and the Corporation for Public Broadcasting (CPB). It revealed that during the 1976-77 school year some 72% of all teachers had instructional television available; of that number, 59% used it. Although the most heavily used source of programming was public television, 37% of all teachers who had ITV available cited the use of nonbroadcast video tape. At the senior high level, 71% of teachers reported video tape as their source of programming. The same study determined that video tape recording and playback equipment was available to more than 870,000 teachers — some 170,000 more than reported using television for classroom instruction.

The study also found that one out of three school districts produced its own video programs. Districts with local production most often reported that the programming was for instructional use (85%), but the majority also produced programs for in-service training and student observation. Many reported using video for student production experience.

Another study, conducted in 1977 by Research Triangle Institute, formed the basis for projections by Children's Television Workshop that 24% of the nation's elementary schools have the capacity to videotape programming off the air and that the overwhelming majority of these schools have at least one television set, usually black and white.

On the basis of these two surveys, it can be estimated that between two thirds and three fourths of the nation's elementary and secondary teachers did not have access to video tape recording and playback equipment as of 1977. Since in general school budgets were tight in the years between 1977 and 1980, it can be assumed that this portion of the market has not grown substantially.

The College Market

The college and university video market, while smaller in absolute numbers than the school market, has moved more quickly to television production.

A 1979 CPB-NCES survey found that 71% of U.S. colleges and universities used television for instructional or other purposes in 1978-79. That survey, which had a 94% response rate, found that 61% of the respondents offered courses via television or used television as an adjunct to traditional methods of instruction. The widest use of video was via closed circuit campus systems, reported by 42% of the respondents, followed by public television (22%), cable systems (9%) and commercial TV stations (7%).

PUBLIC BROADCASTING

Since the present study is concerned with the use of nonbroadcast video, relatively little attention will be devoted to public broadcasting. It is, however, important to recognize the tremendous impact that public broadcasting has had on educational use of video.

This impact has been threefold. First, public broadcasting has gained widespread acceptance as a supplementary teaching tool on all educational levels. The Public Broadcasting Service (PBS), established by the Corporation for Public Broadcasting in 1969 to act as a network linking educational TV stations thoughout the country, broadcasts numerous courses for college credit.

On the elementary/secondary level, PBS provides programming in curriculum areas such as science, English, social studies, languages, art and current events. These programs are watched and discussed during school hours as part of regular classroom lessons, particularly at the elementary school level. Teacher guides, distributed by the station, inform teachers of upcoming programs on such regularly broadcast series as "The Electric Company," "Vegetable Soup," "Tyger, Tyger Burning Bright" and "Word Shop." PBS and the Children's Television Workshop have also authorized limited off-the-air taping of "Sesame Street" by public elementary schools, nonprofit private elementary schools and day care centers. (Off-the-air copies of 1979-80 programs may be used for seven days only and then must be erased.)

Second, public broadcasting has focused attention on at-home television viewing for educational purposes. Programs regarded as instructional as well as entertaining are frequently assigned as "homework." Science programs, such as National Geographic Specials, and adaptations of literary/historical classics (e.g., the "Masterpiece Theater" series) are examples of programs that may be viewed at home and integrated into a study unit.

Third, programs originally broadcast by public television stations are reproduced in cassette form and widely distributed to schools and colleges.

The Corporation for Public Broadcasting reported at year-end 1979 that during fiscal 1978 public broadcasting stations spent $47.7 million for instructional programming for elementary and high school students and an additional $10.5 million for post-secondary services. Of these amounts, approximately $23 million went for actual programming. Of the 282 public television stations operating in 1979, 79 were operated by universities.

In January 1980 PBS was reorganized into three national networks. One of these, the "Green Service," will be responsible for developing instructional programming for both in-school and at-home viewing. Among the new programs planned by the Green Service are a series on minority groups, a series on adolescence and adaptation of evening programs such as "The American Short Story" to daytime college-credit courses.

APPLICATIONS

The primary use of video in education is, of course, instruction. But television is being used increasingly for public relations, in-service training and documentation. Students are also producing programs, ranging from informational tapes to the recording of special events. Traditionally, elementary and secondary schools have provided a market for prerecorded programming, while colleges and universities are more likely to produce their own programs.

Instruction

Educators have become increasingly aware that the current generation of students, brought up on television, is more visually-oriented than print-oriented. Many feel that since students will continue to watch television, it is imperative to integrate this medium into the learning process. As noted previously, video can be used to present entire courses or as a supplement to more conventional modes of instruction.

Elementary/secondary schools

At the elementary and secondary levels, video is most often used as a supplement. A program may be shown to stimulate discussion or a class project, or to present visually information that is also being taught by lecture or textbook. An example of such programming is a 15-cassette series, "The Write Channel," distributed by the Agency for Instructional Television (Bloomington, IN). The series features an animated puppet, R.B. Bugg, as a journalist who needs to improve his writing skills. Directed at primary and intermediate grades, the cassettes show how R.B. Bugg learns to write more interesting, well structured sentences.

In Winnetka, IL, New Trier Township Television supplies educational video programs to 30 schools, with a K-12 student population of 17,000. Programming includes subjects ranging from primary science to high school humanities. In addition to supplying prepackaged programming obtained from outside sources, New Trier Township Television produces its own programs tailored to local needs. Among these programs have been a documentary on King Tutankhamen (timed to coincide with the King Tut exhibit at a nearby museum), a series of 25 biology lab demonstrations, and driver's education tapes.

Schools have found video a particularly effective instructional tool for special education. Programs on practical, day-to-day skills as well as language skills have been used to teach mentally retarded and emotionally disturbed students. Programming to help hearing-impaired students acquire language skills has also proven effective.

Although elementary and secondary schools do rely heavily on professionally produced programming, many institutions also produce their own tapes. Students themselves are often involved in the entire process —

conception, writing, editing, performing and actual production. The Glassboro (NJ) Public Schools, for example, offer four courses for high school students: production techniques, advanced production, acting for television and making film for television. Even elementary school children have participated in production by drawing pictures, writing accompanying narration and acting in television plays.

In many cases, student projects are developed by teachers to improve specific skills, especially language skills such as reading, writing, editing and following directions. The Graphic Expression Reading Improvement System is used in 60 schools in New York State, where students with low reading skills have produced programs and, as a result, improved their reading scores.

Video programs may be produced as a class project in other curriculum areas, such as current events, civics or science. At Edison Intermediate School (Pekin, IL), for example, students in a social studies class produced a program on Mayan Indians and their culture. Students also produce two regular 15-20 minute news shows every other week, featuring stories on newsworthy events and people around the school. Social studies students do the news gathering, writing and reporting; the TV Club (made up entirely of students) handles the production and post-production work.

Colleges and universities

The use of video in higher education has grown tremendously since closed circuit TV was first used in the 1950s to present lectures for oversized classes. Now, entire courses are prerecorded to be presented on television. For example, the University of Arizona Microcampus offers full-credit courses in all types of engineering, as well as mathematics, business and some liberal arts. Students can register in absentia, and tapes, tests and homework assignments are sent to them or to a remote site where the course is presented to a group of students.

At Michigan State University, almost 5% of all course credit hours are video-based. Several large lecture courses, usually on an introductory level, are offered on video tape and shown at locations scattered throughout the campus. When courses are televised, graduate assistants often attend sessions to answer questions. Courses taught primarily via television include Introduction to Economics, Principals of Accounting, General Biology and Introductory Computer Programming.

There are obvious advantages to presenting courses on video tape. Taped courses can be cheaper than live lectures where there are large numbers of students taking the same course, or where the same course is offered every semester; videotaping the lectures once saves an instructor's time and insures that all necessary information is presented to every student. In many instances students who cannot attend classes at a particular hour or location can arrange to view a playback at a more convenient time and place. University libraries frequently have tapes of lectures available for in-library viewing or for circulation. Among the institutions that offer such services are the libraries of the University of Tennessee (Knoxville), the University of Maryland (College Park) and the University of Utah.

Video can also be used in conjunction with more traditional teaching methods. At Cornell University, chemistry and biology lab demonstrations are taped and viewed at the beginning of a lab session. The tapes are available on cassette for later review. Scripts are written by the departments' leading professors, and the tapes present large amounts of material recorded through the microscope. The time savings, for both professors and students, are considerable.

Many Michigan State courses also use video to supplement "live" teaching. One hour a week may be devoted to a taped lecture which all students enrolled in the course attend; the other class hours are devoted to small discussion groups. These small sections, too, may use video as an instructional tool, with students viewing short segments on particular aspects of the subject under study.

Supplementary video programs can allow students to "visit" situations at remote locations rather than take field trips, or may be used to present case studies or dramatizations. Students in such fields as teaching, social work or the performing arts can watch video tapes of themselves in practice situations and analyze their performances.

Students are active producers of instructional programming at the college level. At Burlington County Community College (Pemberton, NJ), for example, students tape presentations for science, speech and theater classes. Students produce regular news programs at a number of colleges and universities.

Postgraduate education is another area of growing application of instructional video. At this level, however, video is used more as a supplement; teaching an entire course via television is rare. Video is particularly effective in teaching science and social science materials. (See Chapter 7 for information on the use of instructional video in medical institutions.)

One innovative approach to the use of instructional video by graduate students has been developed by the California University for Advanced Studies (CUAS), where students must produce a "video thesis" to earn a PhD in education. Individuals with "significant life achievements" who are interested in sharing their knowledge and experience are accepted into the program, which is tailored to each candidate. Depending on the person's background, CUAS recommends a course of study in video planning, script writing, production, post-production and distribution. Once the candidate is experienced with video equipment and procedures, he or she must produce an inexpensive but high quality program about a particular subject. The university will thus develop a lending library, and hopes eventually to be able to offer an alternative degree program through video taped programs.

Other Applications

Orientation

Much as corporate users have turned increasingly to video for employee orientation, so have educational institutions started to use video programs for student orientation. The New Trier Township school district, for example, shows video tapes to give incoming high school students a "tour" of the campus, to demonstrate how to use the library and to describe course offerings within various school departments.

This type of application saves staff time on presentations and ensures that all students receive complete and identical information.

In addition, video is being used for faculty orientation. A tape on employee benefits, for instance, is used at Pennsylvania State University to describe the faculty group insurance plan.

In-service education

In-service teacher education is an area in which locally produced video programming is particularly effective. Such programming can be tailored to the needs of each district or individual institution. The Granite School District's Media Center (Salt Lake City) is one producer of video for in-service education. Teachers have watched tapes on energy issues, the metric system and scientific processes, among other subjects. The media center also runs in-service workshops on video production for teachers.

Information/public relations

At Cornell University video is used largely for public service and information programming. The university's ETV center has produced tapes on such subjects as nutrition, energy conservation, housing and child abuse with information based on university research projects. Documentaries are distributed free of charge throughout New York State and are rented to other organizations in the United States and abroad. Cornell also produces programs on agriculture, home economics and community development for use in its cooperative extension program. These programs are distributed statewide via broadcast or on video cassette.

Pennsylvania State University produces informational programs for both in-school and public viewing. Public service announcements are broadcast on local television.

Vanderbilt University's Television News Archive records evening news broadcasts of the three major commercial networks, as well as local news reports. The Archive also compiles and stores special video reports on topics of local interest. Tapes are made available to other educational institutions on a rental basis.

Elementary/secondary schools also use video for public relations and information purposes. In Danville, IL, the District 118 Central Learning Resources Center cablecasts live coverage of local school board meetings and provides information for parents on various school programs. It also transmits special announcements, such as school closings because of bad weather.

Documentation

Many educational institutions use video to record special events such as guest lectures, cultural presentations and sports. Students often take an active part in these productions, especially at the college/university level. Faculty researchers also use video to document processes and findings.

Recruiting

Video can be an effective medium for student recruiting by colleges. The Collegiate Video Counseling Network (CVCN) in Century City, CA duplicates and circulates tapes made by colleges describing their facilities and programs. Students who cannot make campus visits may view tapes at a local high school or library. CVCN supplies playback equipment and a reference guide to college programs, as well as the tapes themselves.

Continuing education

Professionals who wish to keep abreast of new developments in their fields, or to review particular areas of knowledge, are discovering the benefits of video tapes. Many states require continuing professional education in certain fields, particularly those related to health care. (See Chapter 7.) Professionals may view tapes on home VTRs, at considerable savings in time and cost over attendance at a course or seminar.

Lawyers, too, use video for continuing education. The American Bar Association's Consortium for Professional Education offers tapes for purchase or rental to individuals and organizations. Representative titles are "Dilemmas in Legal Ethics," "Computer-Assisted Legal Research," "Preventing Legal Malpractice" and "Representing a Client before a Grand Jury."

VIDEO PUBLISHERS AND DISTRIBUTORS

The largest audiovisual publishing firms serving the education market include Time-Life Films, Encyclopaedia Britannica Educational Corporation, Learning Corporation of America (LCA), Great Plains National Instructional Television Library (GPNITL) and Films, Inc. These publishers produce some of their own programming but also distribute programs originally presented on broadcast television under licensing agreements with the producers. Programming generally is offered on either a rental or sale basis and some publishers permit customers to duplicate tapes for a fee. Most tapes are available in ¾-inch or ½-inch (Beta or VHS) formats.

Encyclopaedia Britannica Educational Corp. (EBEC)

Encyclopaedia Britannica Educational Corp. (Chicago) publishes a wide variety of programs for use in the schools. Its catalog lists programs in teacher education, early childhood education, special education, language arts, literature/humanities, the arts, science, mathematics, health and safety, social studies, vocational and personal guidance and foreign languages. All are available in any video cassette format or on 16mm or 8mm film and can be either purchased or rented. One series offered is the "Short Story Showcase" for use in literature/humanities classes. Programs include color dramatizations of Edgar Allen Poe's "The Fall of the House of Usher" and Ernest Hemingway's "My Old Man."

Films, Inc.

Films, Inc. (Wilmette, IL) offers film and video programs for use in both elementary and secondary schools. Most are available for purchase or rental in any video cassette format as well as 16mm film. Among the most highly regarded of its programs is "The Age of Uncertainty," a 12-episode series produced by the British Broadcasting Corp. and shown on public television in the United States by KCET-TV, Los Angeles. Others include the 1973 NBC production, "The Forbidden City"; "Sunday Father," a Paul Leaf production featuring actor Dustin Hoffman; "Monet in London," a production of the Arts Council of Great Britain; and "The Adams Chronicles," produced by WNET-TV, New York and originally shown on public television.

Great Plains National Instructional Television

GPNITL (Lincoln, NE) acquires and distributes instructional television programs produced by schools or boards of education throughout the country and by U.S. and British ETV stations. Its 123-page 1980 catalog lists programs for student instruction in elementary/secondary schools and colleges, as well as for in-service teacher education. A total of 150 courses are now offered on film or video cassette. Video cassettes are priced from $140 to $290 for purchase (the price is based on the program length, ranging from 15 minutes to 45 minutes). Five-day cassette rentals cost from $25 to $38, again depending on the program length. Leasing is more expensive if the program is to be shown over closed circuit or cable television systems.

Time-Life Films

The Time-Life Video division of Time-Life Films (Time Inc., New York) markets instructional and entertainment programming to schools, libraries, government agencies and other institutions. Its catalog lists video programming on subjects ranging from social studies and language arts to religion and philosophy, science, health and business. Among current offerings is the "Time-Life Video Reading Efficiency System," featuring television star Bill Cosby. Others include Time-Life Films co-productions with the British Broadcasting Corp., shown in the United States on public broadcasting stations. In addition, the company has acquired the distribution rights to a number of feature films including "From Here to Eternity," "Lawrence of Arabia" and "Bridge on the River Kwai."

Learning Corp. of America

LCA (New York) markets its films and video programs to schools and colleges. Its current catalog lists titles for use in teaching language arts, literature, humanities, art, music, film, American history and ethnic studies, social studies and global studies, world history, environment and human relations. It also offers a number of feature films (transferred to tape on request), edited for educational showing. In addition to the programs for which it has acquired distribution rights, LCA in 1979 announced that it would begin producing programs itself.

Other Publishers or Distributors

Other sources of educational video tapes include McGraw-Hill (New York), American Cable Network (Traverse City, MI) and Video Tape Network (New York). The Agency for Instructional Television (Bloomington, IN) is a nonprofit American-Canadian organization established to coordinate cooperative educational ventures between the states and the provinces. AIT develops, acquires and distributes television and related print materials.

The Intercollegiate Video Clearing House (Miami, FL) is a nonprofit consortium of colleges and corporations dedicated to facilitating the use of video as a supplementary teaching tool. The Public Television Library (Washington, DC), a branch of the Public Broadcasting Service, distributes programs produced by local public television stations.

COPYRIGHT CONSIDERATIONS

A major stumbling block to development of the educational video market — in addition to the chronic shortage of funds — is the schools' inclination to use their own video tape equipment to record programming off-the-air or to duplicate without authorization the video tapes they purchase or rent. In an effort to stem unauthorized duplication, three of the largest publishers, Time-Life, LCA and EBEC, filed suit in 1978 against a New York State school district, the Board of Cooperative Educational Services (BOCES) First Supervisory District in Erie County, NY. The publishers claimed the board had been systematically videotaping off-the-air programs telecast on the Eastern Educational Network and supplying schools in its district with a catalog of taped programs from which they could order. A preliminary injunction won by the three publishers barred the board from futher taping while the case was pending. (The trial date had still not been set as of May 1980.)

There is considerable confusion surrounding the rights of educational institutions to duplicate and circulate copyrighted video materials. One reason for the uncertainty is the vagueness of the Copyright Law of 1976, which became effective on January 1, 1978. The law stipulates four broad criteria for determining "fair use" of a copyrighted work, among them the "purpose and character of the use, including whether such use is of a commercial nature or is for nonprofit educational purposes." However, the interpretation of these criteria has varied widely and will eventually be determined by court tests and licensing arrangements in the marketplace.

Professional bodies, including the Association of Educational Communications and Technology and the Association of Media Producers, are working to develop guidelines for off-the-air copying. A joint policy developed by the Public Broadcasting Service, the Agency for Instructional Television, the Public Television Library and the Great Plains National Instructional Television Library permits schools to record off the air certain "public and instructional television programs distributed by them." (One example is "Sesame Street," mentioned earlier in this chapter.) Copies may be kept for seven days. In addition, AIT has authorized certain agencies to copy and retain its programs for 12 months.

PROSPECTS

Educators are becoming increasingly aware that, since television is here to stay, they should exploit its usefulness as a teaching/learning medium. New developments, including the emergence of the video disc, the growth of interactive television, and expanding cable and satellite transmission, offer intriguing prospects for educational use of video.

Proponents of video discs claim they offer better picture and sound quality, easier storage and retrieval and, ultimately, lower costs than cassette systems. Cassettes, however, can be used to record broadcast programs in the classroom and to produce programming. Burgeoning cable and satellite networks will enable homes and educational institutions, particularly those in remote areas, to receive a wider range of programming than ever before. The educational potential of interactive television, in which the set is linked to a computer, is particularly exciting. A student — even a young child — wishing information on a subject could "call up" material that would otherwise be unavailable to him without extensive library research. The two-way feature could also be used to test students taking a course taught entirely via television.

One factor inhibiting the expansion of educational video in el-hi schools is the comparative lack of programming. Publishers have not found educational programming to be particularly profitable and, in fact, audiovisual sales on the whole have declined markedly since 1975 because of tightening school budgets and a "back to basics" emphasis among parents and educators. In addition, schools using significant amounts of audiovisual materials continue to prefer films to tape. As one educational publisher put it, "We offer everything we have in all the available formats, but 99% of the orders are for 16mm." Some publishers have made special offers to the schools that include a free video tape recorder as an inducement to purchase a given amount of programming. A possible explanation for the continued dominance of film was offered by a media specialist who has encountered strong resistance to video among teachers simply because they prefer the familiar—16mm film—to the unknown.

In general, school use of prerecorded video programs is not expected to increase significantly during the early part of the 1980s. Budget restrictions, declining enrollments and a renewed emphasis on print (i.e., textbook) instruction are likely to remain as inhibiting factors.

At the college level, a majority of institutions are already using video and prospects for increased use are brighter. (At this level, of course, the emphasis is much more on in-house production than on off-the-shelf purchase or rental.) Likely areas of wider use include presentation of lecture courses, public relations and recruiting, laboratory demonstrations and career training. In addition, with the use of video growing rapidly in other markets (particularly business and industry), there is an increasing need for personnel trained in video production. It is likely, therefore, that more educational institutions, especially those with journalism/communications technology programs, will be using video more and more—to teach video.

SURVEY FINDINGS

A total of 393 schools and colleges responded to the *Video Register* survey of video users. Together they comprise the second-largest user group, or 36.1% of the sample. The following is a summary of survey findings for this segment. (Chapter 3 presents data comparing the responses of educational users and other groups to selected survey questions.)

Size of Network

Nearly 46% of the educational users reported having between one and 10 playback locations; more than 30% reported between 11 and 50. About 8% had more than 100. (For additional data and comparison with all users, see Table 3.2.)

Uses of Video

Predictably, the most frequently mentioned video application (cited by 83% of respondents) was student instruction. In-service education was listed by about 67% and continuing education by about 63%. Other areas of heavy use were orientation, public relations and employee training. (For additional data and comparison with all users, see Table 3.3.)

Supervision of Video Services

Nearly 45% of educational users named the media/audiovisual department as the supervisor of video services. This was a far higher percentage than in any other market segment. (For additional data and comparison with all users, see Table 3.4.)

1979 Program Production

More than 32% of educational users reported production of between one and 12 programs in 1979; about 25% were in the 25-59 program range. About 22% produced 60 programs or more. (For additional data and comparison with all users, see Table 3.5.)

1980 Programming

The majority (about 61%) of this group expected to increase production in 1980. Some 26% anticipated increased purchase or rental of off-the-shelf programming. (For comparison with all users, see Table 3.7.)

Hardware Exenditures

About 32% of educational respondents valued their video hardware at under $100,000; nearly one fourth reported equipment valued at $300,000 or more.

More than three quarters of this group planned to purchase new equipment in 1980, with the majority anticipating expenditures of under $50,000. About 6% said they planned to spend $100,000 or more. Nearly one fourth of the respondents did not provide this information. (For comparison with all users, see Tables 3.9 and 3.10.)

Video Budgets

Nearly half of this group failed to report information on total video budgets. About 35% reported budgets of under $100,000; 17% reported budgets of $100,000 or more. (For comparison with all users, see Table 3.12.)

Other Findings

Equipment and facilities

• About 60% of these users owned ¾-inch VTRs; 54% reported having ½-inch equipment. More than 16% had other formats.

- The vast majority (86%) had a video studio.
- More than 80% had editing equipment.
- Only 5.9% had the capacity to duplicate 10 or more tapes.
- More than 85% of educational respondents reported having cameras; about 84% specified studio cameras, 85% portables; 79% color, 78% black-and-white.

Personnel

- More than 90% of this segment reported having a full-time video staff; nearly 56% employed between one and three full-timers. About 64% had part-time staff, usually one or two people.
- Large video staffs (seven or more) were reported by a relatively high percentage (35%) of respondents.
- About 31% reported hiring additional staff for occasional projects. (Some 47% did not answer this question.)
- Nearly 55% of the educational group had a professional video engineer on staff.
- About 41% of these users reported video personnel budgets of less than $100,000; 8% reported personnel budgets of $100,000 or more. (Nearly 33% did not supply data.)

Programming

- Off-the-shelf programming purchases were more frequent in this market segment, with nearly 46% reporting such purchases in 1979. Few users, however, made large purchases (more than 12 programs during the year).
- Nearly 40% rented off-the-shelf programming.
- The great majority of educational users (83%) said they do not contract with outside production companies.
- The highest percentage (18%) of this group estimated a very low "typical" production cost—under $100; 48% placed the cost at under $1000. (Some 40% did not answer the question.)

Anticipated purchases

- Cameras. New camera purchases in 1980 were expected by about 42% of respondents, with 13% planning to spend $10,000 or more.
- VTRs. More than 48% planned to purchase VTRs; 10% expected to spend $10,000 or more.
- Editors. Purchase of editing equipment was planned by about 28% of

these respondents; 8% reported plans to spend $10,000 or more.

• Lights. About 19% of educational users reported plans to buy lights in 1980.

• Audio equipment. About 35% anticipated purchase of audio equipment.

• Other production equipment. Among educational respondents, about 4% planned to purchase a monitor, 5% a character generator, 4% a time base corrector and 5% switchers.

CASE STUDIES

APPALACHIAN STATE UNIVERSITY
Boone, NC 28607

Appalachian State University, located in the mountains of western North Carolina, was a state teachers college for 100 years before it became a university 10 years ago. It enrolls 10,000 students, about half of them at the Boone campus and the other half at centers elsewhere in the state. There are a business school, a college of education and a liberal arts program.

The university has had a video program since 1974. The campus television coordinator directs video activities, which include production of instructional programming, provision of programs from the unit's video library and direct instruction of broadcasting students in video production. There are two studios on campus, one color and one monochrome, and a total of 25 color and black-and-white cameras. Most of the equipment was donated to the school by area broadcast stations, and a continual effort is made to acquire equipment being replaced by broadcast stations.

The video unit produces instructional materials at the request of faculty members. The teacher presents the idea for the program and is responsible for the script, although the video unit does provide scripting assistance if needed. Programming is produced on the basis of the faculty-approved script, and a charge is levied for the materials used. In this manner, 10 programs were produced last year on subjects ranging from tennis to algebra, techniques for teaching reading and the use of research materials. The master tape is retained by the department, with the video library and the faculty member each receiving a duplicate. However, before actual production begins, a search is made for similar programming from outside suppliers; if an appropriate tape is commercially available, it will be purchased.

There is a full-time staff of two persons assigned to the video unit. Two others work on a part-time basis.

The value of Appalachian State's video hardware is estimated at $200,000, and $30,000 was budgeted for the purchase of cameras, VTRs, and editing and audio equipment in 1979. Typically, the amount spent per production is $100 with a maximum expenditure of $1500.

The 1979 video budget was $55,000, of which $25,000 was for staff salaries. The budget increased between 6% and 10% in 1979; it is expected to go up at about the same rate in 1980 and to continue to rise by 6% to 10% over the next five years.

GREENWICH HIGH SCHOOL TELEVISION SERVICES
Greenwich High School, Room 057
Hillside Ave.
Greenwich, CT 06830

The Greenwich school system has a district-wide video services program supervised by a media coordinator and a producer/director who also serves as the television supervisor for the high school. The system includes 10 elementary schools, two junior high schools and one high school. The video effort dates back to 1967 when the district-wide facility was initiated. The high school program started in 1970 when the school itself was constructed.

At the high school there are two studios, a studio/theater seating 75 and a multi-camera production studio. Equipment includes 33 cameras, a Panasonic ¾-inch editing system, Panasonic black-and-white switchers with special effects capability, ½-inch editors and a number of Sony and Panasonic portapaks. Playback equipment includes 12 reel-to-reel units and five ¾-inch cassette units for commercially acquired material. There is also a closed circuit system that reaches 102 classrooms, but only 40 of them have monitors. The high school does a limited amount of closed circuit transmission of special events, mostly by pre-taping the programming.

The high school video facility has two full-time staff members and one part-time employee. The school also makes use of community volunteers who are trained annually to set up, tape and play back video programs.

Ranked in order of importance the video applications at the high school are: student instruction, in-service education, orientation, documentation and employee training.

Students working in the video program have produced video art plus original electronic music. Video also has been used for special education of mentally handicapped or learning-disabled youngsters. As part of a high school career opportunities program, speakers at career workshops have been taped and the school has produced programs on location to illustrate various types of jobs.

As part of its in-service education program, the high school has taped teachers in classroom situations, as well as guidance counselors working with students. Journalism students have produced news and information programming and, for documentation purposes, tapes of guest lecturers. These tapes have been added to the high school's video library as learning resources.

Employee training via video consists for the most part of instructing both teachers and community volunteers in the use of the equipment and in the production of programming.

Purchases of color programming from outside sources are limited, although the high school has purchased some "Nova" productions as well as other programs produced by the Public Broadcasting Service, upon teacher request. The purchasing program is described as "not big — only several thousand dollars per year go into these purchases." Before passage of the 1976 copyright law, the school taped programs off the air. It no longer does so and has destroyed tapes acquired in this manner. However, it continues to tape programs by special agreement from Channel 49, the Connecticut educational television channel with which it is affiliated. Some additional material is acquired in this manner via an agreement with WNET, Channel 13, in Newark, NJ. One difficulty connected with tape acquisition is the lack of current information on what programming is available for purchase. The school's producer/director sees a need for more information and access to available software.

The value of video equipment at Greenwich High School is estimated at $85,000. The school planned to spend $2000 during the 1979-80 school year on the purchase of color monitors and an additional $500 on audio equipment. The total video budget for 1978-79 was $10,500, a 60% increase over the previous year.

The 1979-80 budget represented a 75% decrease from 1978-79 in terms of allocations to the high school, but more funds are being channeled to the junior high and elementary schools as part of a five-year district-wide plan for expanded video services. During this period, the city is expected to start receiving cable TV. The high school anticipates that the cable company will provide public access opportunities and hopes that the company will underwrite the cost of converting the high school facility to color.

NORTHERN NEW MEXICO COMMUNITY COLLEGE
P.O. Box 250
Espanola, NM 87532

Northern New Mexico Community College is located in a rural area 30 miles north of Santa Fe, NM. Its main campus is in Espanola but it has three satellite campuses in the surrounding communities. Total enrollment is approximately 4000 full-time, part-time and night school students. Both academic and vocational courses are offered. The school has been involved with video since early 1977.

There is a studio at the Espanola campus equipped with four black-and-white cameras and four ¾-inch video tape recorders. Plans to spend between $30,000 and $40,000 on new video equipment, including ½-inch VTRs, two color cameras and editing equipment, have been postponed pending action by the state legislature on a request for a new media center in a campus building now under construction. However, some of the funds originally budgeted for new hardware are now being invested in additional video software.

The school's media services department consists of two full-time and two part-time employees who handle projects involving other media in addition to video. Plans to hire a part-time professional video engineer have been delayed, again pending legislative action affecting construction of the new media center.

The college makes considerable use of both rented and purchased video programming. It is more likely to acquire professionally produced programs that can be used in more than one course, rather than tapes treating narrower, more specific topics. Many of the purchased programs have been "how to" in nature. However, the liberal arts departments, particularly English and drama, also make heavy use of video programming. A recent purchase for use in these types of courses was the Shakespeare plays broadcast in 1979 by the Public Broadcasting Service.

During the past year, the media services department produced about six original programs. These included an orientation tape for college employees and a program about the local animal shelter produced by students in a video production course. In addition to this type of programming, the media services department uses video to tape role-playing sessions in career development courses and to tape scenes of plays performed by drama students. Some programming is of a public service nature — for example, the media services staff taped a local fiesta and also taped a number of workshops conducted by public health personnel. The latter tape will be edited into a program for use in future public health projects.

The only tape of a strictly instructional nature to be produced in-house involves a course on radiography (X-Ray techniques). The faculty member teaching the course has invited a number of physicians to give guest lectures. Their lectures will be taped for use in future semesters.

UNIVERSITY OF WISCONSIN, GREEN BAY
Teleproduction Center
Green Bay, WI 54302

The Teleproduction Center at the Unviersity of Wisconsin at Green Bay was planned as a media center when the campus was established 11 years ago but has since become a contract television center to produce video programming for state agencies. It has become involved in the operations of a local broadcast television station and with educational television stations in the state.

The center's productions have ranged from student instruction and in-service education for faculty members to programming for broadcast television. Programs have included studies of mining issues, the history of ship building in Wisconsin, energy conservation and a series on modern food preparation technology. "Encompass," a local public affairs program, is produced weekly and shown twice a week on the local channel, WPNE-TV. Several of the center's programs, including one on American Indians, have been picked up by the Public Broadcasting Service.

In general, programming designed for student instruction is produced for state educational agencies. Productions have included programs to teach French, the social history of Wisconsin, creative dramatics, ethnic folk literature and a series on health. Usually, a program need is first identified and financing must then be found to support production. Although most of the productions are initially broadcast, they eventually wind up on video cassette for classroom use.

All campus classrooms at Green Bay are equipped to play back video programming via 35 VTRs that can be requested as needed. The Teleproduction Center itself has a studio with four color cameras, three of them studio models and one a portable. There is a full-time staff of 22, including five professional video engineers, and a part-time staff of two. During the past year 50 programs were produced. The Teleproduction Center neither purchases nor rents programs from outside sources.

The value of video hardware on hand is estimated at $750,000 and some $60,000 was budgeted for the purchase of cameras, VTRs and audio equipment during the 1979 fiscal year. Production expenses can range from $8000 to $45,000, with $20,000 being a typical cost. The personnel budget alone totals about $350,000.

The Center's budget varies from year to year depending on the number of outside contracts it has entered into. However, the 1979 video budget represents an increase of 11% to 15% over the previous year. The 1980 budget is expected to be the same, but over the next five years a 25% increase is anticipated.

6

Government

Video is being used at all levels of government — local, state and federal. By far the largest user is the federal government, which in 1978 — the last year for which complete figures are available — spent $17.7 million on program production. By far the largest video user within the federal government is the Defense Department, which uses the medium extensively for military education and training.

Since 1978 the U.S. Office of Management and Budget has required each federal agency to submit an annual report on its audiovisual activities to the National Audiovisual Center, which issues a government-wide report on spending for A/V materials and production.[1] It is therefore possible to gauge the extent of video usage at the federal level with some degree of certainty. At the state and local level, however, there are no centralized sources of such information. Therefore, attempts to estimate the scope of video activity are, to a large extent, educated guesses.

Another difficulty in describing government use of video is the overlap between government and other market segments. Departments of

---

[1]The Office of Management and Budget acted to require this report following criticism of federal audiovisual management in the early 1970s by Rep. Barry Goldwater Jr. (R-CA) and subsequent studies by the Office of Telecommunications Policy and the General Services Administration. The criticisms focused on proliferation of audiovisual activities within the government, duplication of production efforts among agencies, poor utilization of government facilities and the lack of information on the volume and cost of federal audiovisual productions.

education, for example, may be classified as educational or government users; veterans' hospitals may be considered medical or government; corporations engaged in government contract work may be seen as business or government users.

These difficulties and limitations should be kept in mind in assessing the information in this chapter.

FEDERAL USE

Table 6.1 lists those agencies of the United States government which in 1978 were engaged in either video production or program acquisition.

The 43 agencies listed in Table 6.1 owned and operated a total of 1496 audio visual facilities, leased 128 others and made use of 69 operated by contractors during 1978. They spent $10.9 million on in-house video production, compared to $1.7 million on programming produced under contract with outside facilities. (See Table 6.2.) An additional $5.1 million was spent for a combination of in-house and contract production. This compares with $23.2 million on in-house and contract motion picture production, 2.1 million on audio tape and record production and $19.1 million on audiovisual programs identified in the National Audiovisual Center's report as "other."

Spending for off-the-shelf video programming was significantly lower. As Table 6.3 shows, federal agencies spent about $3.2 million for 21,008 copies of 8797 programs. This compares with about $6 million for motion pictures, $197,000 for audio tapes or phonograph records and $4.6 million for "other" audiovisual programs.

Defense Department

As previously stated, the Defense Department is by far the largest government user of video. In 1978 it spent more than $8.6 million for 24,397 in-house productions and slightly more than $1.7 million for off-the-shelf programming. Another $263,317 was expended for 236 programs produced by outside contractors.

All Defense Department audiovisual facilities report annually to the Directorate for Audio-Visual Management Policy on their activities. The Directorate also keeps records by title of all A/V materials produced by Defense agencies. The only programs not included in these records are those considered perishable — for example, tapes of weekly briefings that some agencies make for the convenience of those unable to attend. Materials of this nature usually are erased and the tapes re-used.

Approximately 48% of the department's productions are used for training. Defense agencies also use audiovisual materials for the following

Table 6.1: Federal Agencies Reporting Video Tape Production or Purchase, 1978

Agriculture
Commerce
Defense
Energy
Health, Education and Welfare
Housing and Urban Development
Interior
Justice
Labor
State
Transportation
Treasury
ACTION
Agency for International Development
Commission on Civil Rights
Commodity Futures Trading Commission
Community Services Administration
Consumer Product Safety Commission
Environmental Protection Agency
Equal Employment Opportunity Commission
Farm Credit Administration
Federal Communications Commission
Federal Home Loan Bank Board
Federal Maritime Commission
Federal Mediation and Conciliation Services
Federal Trade Commission
General Services Administration
Inter-American Foundation
International Communication Agency
Interstate Commerce Commission
National Aeronautics and Space Administration
National Credit Union Administration
National Foundation on the Arts & Humanities (National Endowment for
    the Humanities)
National Labor Relations Board
National Science Foundation
Nuclear Regulatory Commission
Panama Canal Company
Railroad Retirement Board
Small Business Administration
Tennessee Valley Authority
U.S. Civil Service Commission
U.S. Postal Service
Veterans Administration

Source: *Federal Audiovisual Activity for Fiscal 1978* (Washington, DC: National
    Audiovisual Center, 1979).

Table 6.2: Federal Video Production, 1978

Agency	In-House			Contract			Mixed			
	Titles	Minutes	Cost	Titles	Minutes	Cost	Titles	Minutes	In-House Cost	Contract Cost
Agriculture	70	1,871	$ 14,890	314	2,728	$ 95,420	14	153	$ 36,340	$ 20,080
Commerce	-	-	-	1	5	30,960	-	-	-	-
Defense	24,397	1,094,000	8,647,570	236	28,000	263,317	-	-	-	-
Energy	110	7,280	109,370	11	1,831	54,570	1	17	3,500	1,000
HEW	202	4,400	677,430	279	3,470	536,430	83	884	20,000	230,210
HUD	5	121	24,000	15	374	85,390	-	-	-	-
Interior	1	70	50	2	8	1,000	-	-	-	-
Justice	111	9,840	309,420	4	45	22,690	3	56	3,600	18,000
Labor	115	1,486	183,540	7	351	98,440	11	200	57,430	734,000
State	377	22,620	9,575	-	-	-	-	-	-	-
Transportation	174	20,092	126,400	10	64	122,000	5	75	2,430	46,970
Treasury	105	4,272	381,130	1	30	5,000	12	335	25,800	28,070
ACTION	-	-	-	1	5	210	-	-	-	-
Agency for Int'l Devel.	6	301	14,030	5	228	130,000	-	-	-	-
Comm. on Civil Rights	-	-	-	-	-	-	-	-	-	-
Commodity Fut. Trad. Comm.	-	-	-	-	-	-	-	-	-	-
Comm. Services Admin.	-	-	-	-	-	-	-	-	-	-
Consumer Prod. Safety	2	NA	150	-	-	-	-	-	-	-
EPA	74	5,825	60,000	21	4,723	90,610	-	-	-	-
Equal Emp. Oppt. Comm.	37	1,440	44,550	-	-	-	-	-	-	-

Farm Credit Admin.	–	–	–	–	–	–	–	–	–	–
Federal Commun. Comm.	35	4,261	2,500	–	–	–	–	–	–	–
Federal Home Loan Bank Bd.	8	275	5,680	–	–	–	–	–	–	–
Federal Maritime Comm.	–	–	–	–	–	–	–	–	–	–
Federal Med. & Concs. Ser.	16	233	290	–	–	–	–	–	–	–
Federal Trade Comm.	14	5,040	1,310	–	–	–	–	–	–	–
General Services Admin.	11	480	4,980	–	–	–	–	–	–	–
Inter-Amer. Found.	–	–	–	–	–	–	–	–	–	–
Int'l Comm. Agency	–	–	–	–	–	–	151	5,630	3,388,030	188,010
Int. Commerce Comm.	–	–	–	–	–	–	–	–	–	–
NASA	349	8,149	33,490	520	10,000	164,780	–	–	–	–
Nat'l Credit Union Admin.	NA	NA	139	NA	NA	1,500	–	–	–	–
NFAH (NEH)	–	–	–	–	–	–	–	–	–	–
Nat'l Labor Relat. Bd.	NA	2,400	850	3	1,850	6,290	1	1,850	850	6,290
Nat'l Science Found.	3	60	22,400	–	–	8,000	–	–	–	–
Nuc. Regulatory Comm.	–	–	–	4	4,800	–	–	–	–	–
Panama Canal Co.	–	–	–	–	–	–	–	–	–	–
Rail Retirement Bd.	–	509	–	–	–	–	–	–	–	–
SBA	7	–	9,690	5	150	140	1	30	930	100
TVA	–	–	–	–	–	–	–	–	–	–
US Civil Service Comm.	2	63	11,781	–	–	–	–	–	–	–
US Postal Service	60	234	34,500	–	–	–	–	–	–	–
Veterans Admin.	1,307	86,959	152,250	8	487	1,925	78	1,426	150,310	149,840
TOTALS	27,598	1,282,281	$10,881,965	1,447	59,149	$1,718,672	360	10,656	$3,689,220	$1,422,570

NA: Not available.
Source: *Federal Audiovisual Activity for Fiscal 1978* (Washington, DC: National Audiovisual Center, 1979).

Table 6.3: Off-the-Shelf Purchases of Video Programs
by Federal Agencies, 1978

Agency	Titles	Copies	Cost
Agriculture	9	9	$ 6,080
Defense	2,020	1,688	1,737,590
Energy	17	37	6,420
HEW	1,535	1,157	245,760
HUD	9	561	14,630
Interior	7	22	2,150
Justice	193	13	47,990
Labor	8	8	1,060
Transportation	38	1,812	50,220
Treasury	24	NA	40,510
AID	1	1	270
EPA	7	1	1,841
Federal Maritime Comm.	7	7	920
Int'l Comm. Agency	318	2,604	470,570
Nat'l Labor Relations Bd.	19	1,161	10,710
Nat'l Science Foundation	16	16	—
SBA	5	1	140
U.S. Civil Service Comm.	2	2	320
Veterans Admin.	4,560	11,908	533,130
TOTALS	8,795	21,008	$3,190,321

NA: Not available.
Source: *Federal Audiovisual Activity for Fiscal 1978* (Washington, DC: National
   Audiovisual Center, 1979.)

purposes: public and internal information (8% of programming); recruiting (1%); research, testing and development (12%); intelligence and
reconnaisance (3%); combat readiness (8%); institutional support (6%);
medical and dental information (14%). Although the percentages apply to
all audiovisual materials, a spokesman for the Directorate said it could be
assumed that the same percentages applied to the various categories of
video progamming alone.[2]

[2]Telephone interview with author.

Of the several branches of the armed forces, video is used most widely for training by the army. Production is coordinated by the U.S. Army Training Support Center (USATSC) at Fort Eustis, VA. Programming is geared to individual and small group instruction and encompasses all of the more than 300 different skills required of army trainees. Each tape generally runs between 18 and 20 minutes and is relatively straightforward in nature, making use of special effects, music, etc. only "where appropriate and where it won't detract" from the learning materials. Some programs include a worksheet but most do not. Several titles selected at random from the "Aviation Skills" section of the catalog include "Using the EGT Tester," "Air Craft Inspection Procedures," "Air Craft Rescue and Recover."

Video tapes are produced in the ¾-inch U-Matic format. They are disseminated through a circulation library stocking more than 5000 tapes. Production is handled by 17 production units coordinated by the USATSC which is responsible for the centralized management of all training support material used by the Army. In addition to video, these include simulators, games, training extension courses, slides, photos and films.

Other Federal Agencies

As Tables 6.2 and 6.3 show, none of the other agencies reporting came close to the Defense Department's level of expenditures. The second-largest producer (in terms of funds allocated) was the Department of Health, Education and Welfare; in 1978 HEW spent $677,430 on 202 in-house productions, $536,430 on 279 programs produced by outside contractors and $250,210 on 83 programs produced both in-house and under contract.

The second-largest purchaser of off-the-shelf programming, the Veterans Administration, spent $533,130 for 4560 titles in 1978. (Note that the largest purchaser, the Defense Department, spent more than three times that amount for only 2020 titles.)

STATE USE

The need for video on the state level is not as obvious as it is at the federal. Bureaucracies are much smaller, and except in specific agencies, employees are not spread throughout large geographical areas. The use of video for training and communication is strongest among those agencies with personnel dispersed thoughout the state — for example, law enforcement and transportation. The New York State Transportation

Department, for example, uses video training materials for distribution to highway maintenance personnel for instruction on such matters as equipment operation and maintenance, tree pruning and removal, etc. Video also is used by the transportation departments in California and Minnesota. Arizona and Texas are among the states whose police or public safety agencies utilize video for training and communication of new directives, policy, etc.

State law enforcement agencies also produce a variety of educational programs. For example, the New Jersey Division of Narcotic and Drug Abuse Control, a statewide agency, adopted a plan in 1972 to use video for general communication and training. It has taped programs on drug abuse prevention, drug and alcohol treatment, minority issues, women's issues and drug and alcohol workshops for use in public education efforts. Video has also been used to tape counseling sessions, seminars, meetings and workshops.

In New York State the Department of Correctional Services in Albany has established a fully equipped color television studio operated by inmates at correctional institutions and student interns from the State University of New York. It produces programming for state agencies, public service groups and such nongovernmental clients as Citibank, the United Methodist Council and the American Red Cross. The tapes offer training and communications for state prison inmates and correctional system employees on such matters as employee orientation and benefits, classification of fingerprints, hostage negotiations, conversational Spanish and procedures for temporary release, as well as a bilingual social studies program for inmates.

Programming for nonstate agencies includes public service announcements for the National Alliance of Businessmen, a boating safety course for the U.S. Coast Guard, a tape on patient interviewing techniques for the Capitol District Psychiatric Center and recruiting tapes for the U.S. Army Reserves.

Video in the Courts

One notable new and growing use of video in government, particularly at the state level, is the taping of testimony and depositions to be presented in court. The introduction of video as a significant feature in the courtroom was made in 1971 in Sandusky, OH, at the instigation of Judge James L. McCrystal. Although video had been used earlier for the taping of depositions of witnesses who could not be present at trials, the 1971 date is notable because it marks the first trial in which all testimony was presented on video tape. The tape was prerecorded and then edited by Judge

McCrystal to delete all inadmissable questions, answers and comments. Between the lawyers' opening and closing arguments, which were presented live, the jurors watched the taped testimony.

According to Judge McCrystal, this use of video in the courtroom offers numerous advantages to both the litigants and the taxpayers. Among them are:

• Trials can be conducted in one-third to one-half the time.

• The procedure virtually eliminates the possibility of a mistrial because the jury never hears inadmissable comments, questions or answers.

• Judges can make better use of their time because they need not be physically present while the jurors hear testimony.

• There are no postponements or continuances because of a witness' or an attorney's inability to appear.

• Cases that are often settled just prior to or during a civil trial are likely to be settled at the time of taping—before a trial date has even been set. Thus, docket congestion is reduced.

• Costs of trials can be significantly reduced.[3]

Since the 1971 Sandusky trials, two other states, Wisconsin and Indiana, have permitted entire trials to be videotaped. Other states have made varied use of video tape in the courtroom: in California, Maryland and Florida, police and attorneys have shown tapes of confessions, line-ups and even the trail of blood leading to scenes of crime. Two U.S. presidents have testified on tape in trials affecting them: President Gerald R. Ford recounted on tape what he saw and heard when an attempt was made on his life in September 1975 for use in the trial of Lynette (Squeaky) Fromme. And President Jimmy Carter testified on tape to be used at the trial of Georgia State Sen. Culver Kidd.

A related use of video in the legal profession has been the re-enactment and taping of landmark case trials at Boston University School of Law. Whenever possible, the same judge, counsel and witnesses who participated in the original trials are used. The aim of the project is to develop a video tape library of key cases that have shaped recent law.

At present, however, the most extensive use of video tape in the courtroom remains the presentation of testimony of witnesses who, for reasons of health, geography or other obstacles, cannot be present personally. (See, for example, the case study of the Delaware County Courts later in this chapter.) Some states require transcriptions or

---

[3]James L.McCrystal, "Videotape Trials: A Primer," *Judicature,* Vol. 61, No. 6 (December/January 1978), pp. 250-256.

typewritten copies of taped depositions. However, the Commissioners on Uniform State Laws have recommended that the states adopt a statute or court rule permitting the use of videotaped depositions without such back-up materials.

Other State Agencies

At the state level, video is widely used by education departments which produce programming for use in the schools. This chapter includes a case study of the New York Education Department Media Services agency, which produces a wide range of programming in collaboration with other agencies for distribution to schools in New York State and throughout the nation. Education departments in Florida, Maryland, Michigan, Missouri, Ohio, North Carolina and Wyoming also produce video programming.

Other state government agencies that make use of video include public health, youth services, agriculture, environmental and library departments.

LOCAL USE

At the local level, video use is most widespread in the schools and is appropriately classified within the education rather than government market. Aside from the schools, video activities are most likely to be found locally among agencies with an on-going need to train large groups — specifically, police or fire departments. (Two of the case studies in this chapter describe video use by local police departments in New York City and Fort Worth, TX.) Many of these video training efforts were initiated as a result of grants funneled through the states from the federal Law Enforcement Assistance Administration (LEAA). Unfortunately, no figures are available on how many LEAA grants were awarded to establish video programs. The LEAA itself could provide no information on how much of its grant money went for police department video training activities.

In addition to the use of video for training, police departments often tape local events — parades for example — for documentation and to analyze whether or not their crowd control or traffic procedures were appropriate to the situation or could be improved. Some tapes produced by police departments are made available to the public as part of their community relations efforts — tapes of community events, for instance, may be loaned to local groups for viewing by their members.

Video is also a communication aid for police departments. New directives from police chiefs, new policies or procedures may be presented to officers via video tape at daily briefings as a means of insuring that all members of the department get the same message.

Fire departments, which apparently have not yet adopted video as widely as have police departments, have similar needs for training and documentation. The Wilmington (DE) Bureau of Fire Prevention adopted video for training in 1972 and has since it used for a variety of purposes. Fire investigators, for instance, use video to gather evidence aimed at determining how a blaze started and what factors were responsible for its spread. Similarly, fires in progress have been taped for later use in evaluating procedures and analyzing such factors as hose placement, ladder work and traffic control. Some programming has been developed for public education on such matters as fire prevention, fire safety and the work of the fire department.

PROSPECTS

The proliferation of video activities at the federal level of government testifies to its usefulness as a training and communications tool where needs are greatest — among users with large, geographically dispersed staffs, a frequent turnover of personnel, and the need to continuously inform people of new facts or procedures. Certainly the extent of video use by the Defense Department supports this thesis.

A similar pattern prevails at the state and local level — usage is greatest among agencies with on-going training needs and large numbers of employees. Other local agencies, especially those with limited contact with the public, smaller staffs and only sporadic training needs, are less likely to opt for video.

It would appear that the prospects for growth at the local level are most promising among those governmental units with greatest responsibilities for public education and whose employees are in daily and personal contact with the public. Health departments, for example, certainly could make use of video in clinics and as part of health education activities. Similarly, social service or human resources departments are other likely prospective users of video to serve training, public education and community relations functions. These agencies conceivably could become customers for off-the-shelf programming, especially on such issues as health, drug and alcohol abuse, nutrition, etc. Other chapters in this study have mentioned the impact of cable television on distributing programming. Certainly, governmental agencies might enlarge their public education and community relations activities through a local cable system's public access channel.

The future of video use at the state level is more difficult to foresee, just as the extent of current activity is impossible to assess. Although the pattern developed to date — heaviest use among departments of education and those concerned with law enforcement — probably will remain unchanged, some increased use should be observed (as was forecast for local governments) among those agencies with public education responsibilities and those whose services must be dispersed throughout the state.

Federal activity is expected to continue to expand along current patterns of use, although video should continue to erode reliance on other A/V formats.

SURVEY FINDINGS

Ninety-two federal, state and local government agencies responded to the *Video Register* survey, representing 8.5% of the total sample. The following is a summary of survey findings for this segment. (Chapter 3 presents data comparing the responses of government users and other groups to selected survey questions.)

Size of Network

Nearly half of the government respondents had between one and 10 playback locations; 37% reported between 11 and 50. Less than 6% had more than 100. (For additional data and comparison with all users, see Table 3.2.)

Uses of Video

The vast majority of respondents—more than 80%—used video for training. In-service education and orientation, both closely allied with training, were cited by about 65% of these users. Video as a public relations tool was reported by a higher percentage of government organizations (60.3%) than any other responding group. (For additional data and comparison with all users, see Table 3.3.)

Supervision of Video Services

Within government agencies either the training or education department was most often responsible for video services. (For additional data and comparison with all users, see Table 3.4.)

1979 Program Production

Government respondents most often reported that they had produced between 1 and 12 video programs in the last 12 months, with 47% falling into this category. Just over 41% produced more than 12 programs; 14% said they had produced 60 or more. In this group, 12% did not report producing any programs in 1979. (For additional data and comparison with all users, see Table 3.5.)

1980 Programming

The majority (60%) of government users expected to increase video production in 1980; 26% expected to produce the same number of programs. Only about 15% anticipated increases in off-the-shelf purchases or rentals. (For comparison with all users, see Table 3.7.)

Hardware Expenditures

About 31% of government respondents valued their video hardware at under $100,000; about 23% reported having $300,000 or more in equipment. Nearly one fourth of the respondents did not answer this question.

Nearly two thirds of government users reported plans to purchase new equipment in 1980, but the great majority expected only modest expenditures—under $50,000. A little more than 8% said they planned to spend $100,000 or more. A large number of government users did not provide this information. (For comparison with all users, see Tables 3.9 and 3.10.)

Video Budgets

More than half of this group failed to report information on video budgets. About 25% reported budgets of less than $50,000; 14% reported budgets of $100,000 or more. (For comparison with all users, see Table 3.12.)

Other Findings

Equipment and facilities

• Half of all government respondents owned ¾-inch VTRs, and 39% reported ½-inch equipment. About 8% had other formats.
• More than two thirds (69%) of these users had a video studio.
• More than 70% had editing equipment.
• Only 5.4% had the ability to duplicate 10 or more tapes at a time.
• More than 81% of these respondents reported having cameras; about 70% had studio cameras, 81% had portables; 70% had color, 60% black-and-white.

Personnel

- Over 80% of government users said they had full-time video personnel; more than half of these reported between one and three full-timers. Forty-five percent had part-time staff, usually one or two.
- Large video staffs (seven or more) were reported by 27% of government respondents.
- Only about 16% of this segment reported hiring additional staff on a project basis. (Well over half did not answer this question.)
- More than 55% of these users did not have a professional video engineer on staff.
- The vast majority of reported video personnel budgets were under $100,000, with a concentration in the $25,000-$49,999 range. (Nearly half the government participants did not report these data.)

Programming

- Less than 30% of government users reported purchases of off-the-shelf video programming.
- Even fewer—under 20%—rented off-the-shelf programming.
- Nearly three quarters of government respondents said they do not contract with outside companies for production assistance.
- The "typical" expenditure on a video production is relatively modest. About 27% placed the cost at under $1000; less than 10% reported a typical cost of $2000 or more. (The majority of users did not respond to this question.)

Anticipated purchases

- Cameras. New camera purchases are planned by about 40% of government respondents in 1980, with 19% planning to spend $10,000 or more.
- VTRs. Purchases of VTRs were also anticipated by 40% of this group; 10% had a budget of $10,000 or more.
- Editors. Nearly 21% anticipated 1980 purchases of editing equipment, with 8% reporting a $10,000 or larger budget for such purchases.
- Lights. Planned purchase of lights was indicated by about 14% of the government users.
- Audio equipment. Roughly 27% said they would purchase audio equipment in 1980.
- Other production equipment. Of government respondents, 5% planned to purchase a monitor, 4% a character generator, 3% a time base corrector, 3% a switcher, and 1% a special effects generator.

Anticipated budgets

• More than 20% of government respondents anticipated a budget increase in 1980; 37% expected budgets to rise over the next five years. (About half of the users did not answer these questions.)

CASE STUDIES

ARIZONA DEPARTMENT OF PUBLIC SAFETY
P.O. Box 6638
Phoenix, AZ 85005

The Arizona Department of Public Safety began using video in 1971. Its primary use is for training and police recruit instruction, but the department also uses video programming to communicate news and information, for public relations and for employee orientation. It has a network of 20 viewing stations, serves 15 additional locations equipped by the Arizona Law Enforcement Officers Advisory Council, and circulates its programming among other police organizations throughout the state.

The department has a studio equipped with three studio and six portable cameras. Five of the cameras are color and four are black-and-white. The studio has electronic editing equipment but lacks the capacity to duplicate more than 10 tapes in-house.

Two full-time and six part-time employees make up the staff of the video unit, but there is no professional video engineer among them. During the past year, the department produced 36 programs and purchased an additional 25 from outside sources.

For the most part, programming consists of instructional material concerned with various phases of police work. One recent program taught officers how to fill out the tags attached to bodies of accident and crime victims; another explained FBI and army tactics for entering buildings where hostages are being held; a third described autopsy procedures. Some of these tapes are shown as segments in a magazine-type format, while others are "single shot" efforts.

There is also a series entitled "Update" that has a news format and is designed for management communication. Occasionally, the department uses video as part of its public relations/community relations effort; for instance, it made a tape of a local street fair for presentation at community meetings.

The department places the value of its video equipment at $150,000.

Under a new reorganization plan it will begin to upgrade its studio and replace outmoded equipment with new cameras, VTRs and editing equipment. A total of $5000 was budgeted for new purchases during the 1979 fiscal year.

DELAWARE COUNTY COURTS
Front and South Sts.
Media, PA 19063

The Delaware County Courts are the only courts within the state of Pennsylvania to maintain an in-house video production operation. Television is used by the courts primarily to present the testimony of witnesses who for some reason — ill health, travel plans, etc. — cannot testify in person during trials. In addition, the video department tapes crime scenes so that jurors can view them without leaving the courtroom. Some 125 productions for these two purposes are made annually. The department also tapes meetings, seminars and conferences for viewing by members of the bar association or court employees who cannot be present.

The courts have five ½-inch VTRs at four locations. The video unit has its own studio and three cameras — one studio and two portables. It also has ½-inch reel-to-reel editing capacity. There are three full-time staff members, but no professional video engineer. All production is handled in-house and no packaged programming is purchased or outside contractors utilized in program production.

The Delaware County Courts have been engaged with video since 1973. The hardware on hand is valued at $75,000 and approximately $5000 has been allocated for the purchase of additional VTRs during the coming year. An estimated $300 is spent per production, excluding staff salaries. The total video budget is $40,000, of which $28,000 goes toward salaries. The 1979 budget represents a 6% to 10% increase over the previous year's, and comparable increases are projected for the coming five years.

FORT WORTH POLICE DEPARTMENT
1000 Calvery St.
Fort Worth, TX 76107

The Fort Worth Police Department's video unit began operating in mid-1979, with a grant from the Law Enforcement Assistance Administration for the purchase of video equipment and the establishment of a video facility for police training and communication. The department purchased

16 VTRs, six of them ¾-inch units and 10 of them ½-inch machines. A storage room at police headquarters was converted into a studio and equipped with four cameras—one studio model and three portables. Three of the four are color cameras.

There is one full-time police officer in charge of both production and distribution and two others who work with the video unit on a part-time basis. In addition, volunteers from the police department have helped with studio construction, camera work and scripting.

Initially, video programming was intended for use in recruit instruction. But because the police chief has decided that officers can no longer be pulled off duty for additional training, video will be used instead to communicate changes in policy and procedures for presentation to police officers during roll call.

As part of the department's community relations effort, the video unit recently filmed a local parade and will make the tape available to business associations for replay at meetings. It has also produced a program in conjunction with the local fire department as part of the observance of "National Fire Fighters Memorial Day."

Because the program is so new, no funds have yet been requested for additional equipment. The video budget is $50,000, of which $25,000 goes for staff salaries. Production expenditures are negligible and involve only the cost of tape and the amortization of the equipment.

NEW YORK CITY POLICE DEPARTMENT
235 East 20th St.
New York, NY 10003

The New York City Police Department uses video for training, information, documentation and surveillance. Its use of video dates back to 1974 when, with the support of a grant from the Law Enforcement Assistance Administration, it purchased the equipment needed for production and distribution. Since then no additional funds have been available to the department to update or upgrade its equipment and none are expected to be forthcoming as a result of the financial plight of New York City and budgetary restrictions imposed on the Police Department.

Each of the city's 73 precincts is equipped with a ¾-inch video tape recorder for playback of video cassettes. Each cassette circulates on a 45-day cycle and approximately 10 cassettes reach each precinct per year. Each one contains a series of one- or two-minute segments designed to inform officers of changes in procedures, instruct them in new techniques or tactics, and advise them of changes in the law and/or rulings by the police commissioner. Examples of topics presented include how to take cover and concealment in combat situations, carrying injured victims, diplomatic immunity, the dangers and treatment of human bites, the rights of the accused in pre-trial publicity, how to evacuate a building in a bomb scare, etc.

Using video for documentation, the department taped the entire New York City visit of Pope John Paul II. The tape was also used as a means of evaluating departmental performance and as a critique of surveillance techniques.

Because of the city's fiscal problems, the police department had no new recruits for a five-year period in the late 1970s and therefore produced no video programming designed for student instruction. However, in 1979 recruits again began entering the department and new programming will be designed for their training. (No specific plans had been formulated in early 1980.)

The video facility also produces some special programming upon request. For example, it produced one on the modus operandi of "Son of Sam" for the chief of detectives during the search for the killer of a number of young women in New York during 1978. It also produced a 12-minute program on the responsibilities of officers responding to hostage situations and another on safe-cracking for use by the crime-scene unit.

The department is equipped with 150 ¾-inch VTRs as well as four ½-inch machines and four 1-inch Ampex VPR-7950s. When the video effort was inaugurated a studio was installed at the police academy. Today, the video staff consists of seven full-time employees, all of them police officers who act alternately as scriptwriters, actors, cameramen or editors. No outside professionals or contractors are used.

The police department produces about 70 programs per year and expects this number to increase. No programming at all comes from outside sources. The value of video equipment is approximately $600,000 and although an additional $20,000 has been requested for the purchase of additional cameras and VTRs, the size of the budget both for new equipment and continued operation is difficult to predict with any degree of certainty.

NEW YORK STATE EDUCATION DEPARTMENT
Bureau of Mass Communications
Cultural Education Center
Albany, NY 12230

The New York State Education Department co-produces video programming for use in the schools in cooperation with governmental and
nongovernmental agencies which provide the financing. It has been
engaged in video production for 17 years. In 1979, it produced an
estimated 40 different programs with the actual work handled by outside
production companies. Programming is designed for use in student
instruction, continuing education, documentation and in-service education
and is available, free of charge, upon request from educational television
stations and boards of education within New York State. In addition to its
own programs, the department's catalog lists some 60 programs acquired
from outside sources which it makes available as part of its video services.
The catalog is distributed, free of charge, on request to schools and other
organizations throughout the country.

Among the organizations with which the Education Department has
co-produced programming are the United Nations, National Instructional
Television, the Ontario Educational Communications Authority, the
Canadian Broadcasting Corp., the Metropolitan Museum of Art, the
Asian Broadcasting Union, Film Modules, Inc., the Asia Society and a
number of federal government agencies.

All told, there are more than 1500 programs available through the
Education Department. The user merely prepares an order form and
submits a blank tape in the requisite format in order to receive the program
desired. The formats used include 2-inch quadruplex, 1-inch helical
Ampex, ½-inch EIAJ-I and U-Matic video cassette.

The 1980 catalog lists the following among available programs:
"Children of the World," a nine-part series for elementary school students,
co-produced with the Canadian Broadcasting Corp. and UNICEF;
"Emerging Playrights," a series designed to further understanding of
contemporary theater produced by the Education Department; "Problems
Are for Solving," a guide for in-service or pre-service use by elementary
school teachers, curriculum and instructional administrators and teacher-
training institution faculty and students; "Footsteps," a series of 20 half-
hour videotaped programs examining everyday situations and problems
confronting parents of young children, produced by the Department of
Health, Education and Welfare; and "Energy: Two Ways of Life," a
co-production with UNICEF designed to illustrate how energy consump-
tion differs in industrialized and non-industrialized nations.

Despite the fact that most of its production work is done under contract with outside sources, the department has a two-camera studio, a full-time staff of seven, electronic editing equipment and equipment needed to duplicate in excess of 10 tapes. It has seven playback machines of varying formats, including ¾-inch, ½-inch and quadruplex equipment. The total value of the hardware on hand is placed at $200,000 and, although no separate budget exists for new equipment, the department does plan to purchase additional ½-inch VTRs in both VHS and Betamax formats in conjunction with a federally funded project. The annual video budget varies according to the production schedule and the funds received from the federal government and other agencies with which there are co-production projects under way or in prospect.

7

Medicine

Television has a long history in medical institutions, starting in 1937 when an operation was shown over closed circuit television at Johns Hopkins University Hospital. Today, most U.S. medical schools use television for student instruction, and video is fast becoming accepted as an effective means of continuing education for physicians and other health professionals.

Traditionally, medicine has been quick to adapt technological advances — computers, audio tape and other innovations. Indeed, the medical breakthroughs most heralded in recent years have involved new and costly hardware — CAT (computerized axial tomography) scanners, ultrasound, etc. Given the receptivity of the health professions to new technology and new uses of existing technology, it is hardly surprising that video is firmly ensconced in this segment of the market, with excellent prospects for the future.

APPLICATIONS

Surprisingly, perhaps, the most frequent uses of video in medical institutions do not differ markedly from those of other educational institutions and some segments of the business and industrial market. Primary applications are in-service education, continuing education, staff training and student instruction. (In some cases, particularly in teaching hospitals, these may be one and the same.) Uniquely medical applications—which in many instances are still very limited—include the taping of surgical procedures, remote diagnosis and consultation, patient education, research and actual treatment.

Student Instruction

The principal use of video in medical schools is for student instruction. The nature of this instruction, however, differs from that in other educational settings. The emphasis is not on the viewing of prerecorded programming but on taping student performance for later faculty evaluation and criticism. Most often, a student will be taped while interacting with a patient—eliciting a medical history, discussing the course of treatment or explaining tests and physical examinations to be administered.

The case studies at the conclusion of this chapter illustrate the use of video for student instruction.

Continuing Education

A total of 22 states now require physicians to present evidence periodically of continued medical education (CME), and most medical associations and specialty boards have minimum CME standards which their members must meet. In addition, a number of states require continuing education for practitioners in medically related fields, such as nursing, optometry and pharmacy.

Video is being used increasingly for such education. Medical conferences and seminars, for example, are taped for presentation or distribution to those who cannot attend. Substituting a video program for personal attendance at such a meeting is seen as a particularly cost-effective means of satisfying CME requirements. One estimate places the loss of physician income incurred by closing an office for two weeks to attend a medical convention at $5400, not counting travel expenses.

A number of specialty boards and professional associations, as well as the American Medical Association and medical schools throughout the country, have produced CME programming for health specialists. There are also a few commercial producers of programming for institutions and individual users in homes and offices. (More information on CME programming appears later in this chapter.)

Surgical Procedures

The application that most quickly comes to mind when video is discussed in conjunction with medicine is the taping or transmitting of new, difficult or highly specialized surgical procedures. Ironically, however, this is probably the least frequent application of video in the medical sphere. As one speaker at an International Television Association seminar in the fall of 1979 noted, the vast majority of physicians, let alone medical students, are not an appropriate audience for this type of programming: out of the entire medical profession, the number of qualified specialists who would constitute the potential audience for any given procedure is relatively small. Of the nation's 348,443 practicing physicians, less than a third are in the surgical specialties. Table 7.1 presents a breakdown of the number of active surgeons by specialty and demonstrates that even the largest group, the general surgeons, has only 32,292 practitioners.

Table 7.1: Surgical Specialties

Anesthesiology	13,182
Colon and rectal surgery	673
General surgery	32,292
Neurological surgery	2,985
Obstetrics and gynecology	22,294
Opthalmology	11,455
Orthopedic surgery	11,814
Otolaryngology	5,864
Plastic surgery	2,351
Thoracic surgery	2,036
Urology	6,903
Total surgical specialists	111,849

Source: *Health Resources Statistics,* 1976-77 edition (Washington, DC: Department of Health, Education and Welfare, National Center for Health Statistics, n.d.).

Telemedicine

Perhaps the most dramatic use of video in medicine is for remote diagnosis, consultation and patient examination. Television enables a physician who may be hundreds — or even thousands — of miles away to examine a patient, consult with a colleague or microscopically examine blood smears and other slides. Only a few demonstrations of how video can be used in this manner have taken place.

Two pilot projects have been conducted in Boston by Dr. Kenneth D. Bird of the Massachusetts General Hospital. Bird first explored the use of television for remote diagnosis and consultation during the late 1960s when he was in charge of the medical facility at Boston's Logan Airport. Under a $350,000 three-year demonstration grant secured by Dr. Bird from the U.S. Public Health Service, doctors at Massachusetts General Hospital examined more than 500 patients at the airport. Dr. Bird describes a typical case:

> If a patient came to the airport medical station complaining about his elbow, a nurse could take the history, do a preliminary examination and then bring him into an examining room. The doctor, several miles away, could operate the cameras in the examining room by remote control. He could get to know the patient, ask questions, have the nurse manipulate the arm to see how the elbow was affected, and zoom in to look at it. The only thing missing was color and that's not so important. The nurse could accurately report color changes to the doctor.[1]

The Logan demonstration, considered successful, was terminated when the grant expired. Dr. Bird then received a grant from the Veterans Administration for a demonstration video link between the psychiatric service at Massachusetts General and the Bedford, MA Veterans Administration Hospital, a 1000 bed neuropsychiatric facility. This demonstration was particularly successful, reports Dr. Bird:

> We found that "telepsychiatry" draws patients out faster than face-to-face psychiatry. There have been all sorts of reasons suggested for why it happened.... We think it has to do with territorial rights and what we call proxemics, the understanding of the way an individual interacts with the space around him. We had a beautiful system with remote zoom in and zoom out capacity so the doctor could get a close-up of the patient's face. It was an amazing demonstration. You know, the psychiatrists say, "Put something between me and my patient and you destroy the relationship," but that simply didn't happen.

---

[1]Telephone conversation with the author.

That project, too, ended when the demonstration grant ran out. In the winter of 1980, Dr. Bird set up a third telemedicine demonstration, this one between Massachusetts General and a Boston nursing home, for remote examination and diagnosis.

Eventually, he foresees, television will link "superdocs" at major teaching hospitals with practitioners elsewhere, thus expanding access to quality medical care. "This way, if you need Michael DeBakey, you can hook up a conference circuit. He wouldn't have to go to Panama to examine the Shah (of Iran) before surgery." Today, explains Dr. Bird, "it's impossible to get the superdocs out of their own hospitals. It's the travel time that does them in, even if they're just going to a hospital across town. By the time they drive there and find a parking place and examine the patient and get back to their own hospital, half the day is gone. With telemedicine they'd never have to leave the office."

One obstacle to this kind of telemedicine is the money needed to establish such a service. Ultimately, the financial problem may be resolved by "narrowcasting" on cable television, using a limited channel to which only certain subscribers have access. If a medical institution became part of an area cable system, it would not have to expend the resources necessary to establish its own system.

Patient Education

A growing use of video in the medical sphere is for patient education. Such programming may be designed to inform a patient about procedures to be performed or about the causes and treatment of specific medical conditions. Many hospitals now have video tapes shown to all new mothers to demonstrate basic aspects of infant care — how to bathe the baby, how to change a diaper, etc., as well as programs on breast feeding and contraception.

Still another emerging use of video is for out-patient education, particularly for patients who are uneducated and might have difficulty reading written instructions on medication, diet, etc. Viewing a television program that explains their condition and the type of treatment prescribed can give these individuals a better understanding than even a conversation with a physician, nurse or social worker. This is especially true if the patient is too nervous or ill-at-ease to fully comprehend the explanation. The use of video in this setting can save valuable physician, nurse or other health workers' time and can provide a fuller, more graphic explanation than may be possible when time is at a premium and other, more urgent, cases are waiting.

Other Applications

In the areas of staff training and orientation, programming in medical institutions differs only in subject matter from programming for employees in business and industry, education and government. For example, a new lab assistant or technician might be instructed via television how to clean a catheter or how to operate various pieces of equipment.

Additional hospital uses of video include patient entertainment, public relations, record keeping and research (taping the behavior of laboratory animals under study). In fields such as psychiatry and psychology, video has been used for diagnosis, treatment and documentation. For example, therapists have taped group or family therapy sessions in order to evaluate progress over a period of time.

Satellite Transmission

As part of an experimental program in decentralized medical education, the University of Washington in Seattle broadcast 350 television programs via satellite to centers in the states of Washington, Alaska, Montana and Idaho. The experiment, called WAMI (after the initials of the participating states), was an attempt to provide a broader range of educational opportunities to students, to recruit medical students and to upgrade health care in mountainous and inaccessible regions.

Between 1974 and 1979, WAMI used communications satellites to provide two-way video communication between Seattle and the Alaska, Montana and Idaho centers. Early transmissions were via the ATS-6 satellite, but the majority of the programs (219 regularly scheduled broadcasts between 1977 and 1979) were transmitted via the Communications Technology Satellite (CTS).

Some of the programs were designed to facilitate the medical school admissions process. Several minority recruiting programs to encourage Indians and Eskimos to enter the health sciences were prepared and conducted by the dean for student affairs. Live demonstrations of course segments were also sent to students at peripheral medical school sites. These were considered particularly successful and several were taped for later use. Another aspect of the video experiment considered of great value was medical consultation between doctors in Seattle and those at the outlying centers.

The satellite itself became inoperative in November 1979, ending this aspect of the WAMI program. Grants from the four states involved, which had financed the bulk of the transmissions, have expired, and prospects for future financing are uncertain.

OFF-THE-SHELF PROGRAMMING

Prerecorded video tapes for use in medical institutions are available from a variety of commercial and noncommercial sources. As has been mentioned, many professional medical associations produce and distribute programs on video tape for use in continuing education. Among those that provide such programming are the American Society of Clinical Pathologists, the AMA, the American Hospital Association, the Ear Research Institute and the National Medical Audiovisual Center.

In addition, prerecorded programming is produced and distributed at little or no cost to users by many of the large pharmaceutical companies. For this reason commercial publishers of videotaped medical programming have made few inroads into the market: they simply cannot compete with firms that supply programs free or at nominal cost. (Among the pharmaceutical companies that distribute video programming are Abbott Laboratories, Ayerst, Davison Gecht, Eli Lilly, Ethicon, Inc. and the Upjohn Corp.) The few commercial publishers that remain in the market include J.B. Lippincott, which publishes a wide selection of materials for use in nursing schools as well as a limited amount for medical and other health professions schools, and McGraw-Hill Medical Publications.

One especially active publisher in the field has been the Emory Medical Television Network (Atlanta, GA), formerly the Georgia Regional Medical Network. It provides video programming to 150 subscribers to its catalog, as well as tapes for rental and purchase by nonmember institutions. Membership costs $990 per year for large hospitals and $495 per year for smaller institutions. The fee entitles members to borrow as many tapes as desired from the circulating library and to make one copy of any tape for use within their own institutions. Emory's 1979-80 catalog lists more than 400 programs in virtually every field of medicine.

The market for continuing medical education materials has to a great extent been supplied by medical institutions and professional organizations and therefore has, to date, offered only limited opportunities for commercial publishers. However, the Network for Continuing Medical Education (NCME) markets such materials to 700 hospital subscribers and some 1000 individual physician subscribers. It distributes one 60-minute cassette to subscribing hospitals every two weeks. Individual physician subscribers can purchase six NCME telecourses per year for home or office use for $275 or rent the same six for $210. Additional courses are available for purchase at $75 or for rent at $58. All are in ½-inch video cassette format (either Beta or VHS), although they will be supplied, upon request, in other formats (and priced by format).

Among the telecourses offered by NCME for home use in 1980 were an introduction to the field of adolescent medicine, a guide to initial emergency room care of automobile accident patients, a guide to treatment of adult-onset diabetes and a review of the basic principles of immunology. There are also a variety of short tapes running 15 to 20 minutes on topics including the management of frostbite, diagnosis and management of hypercalcemia, how to evaluate non-traumatic shoulder discomfort, etc. All courses qualify for continuing education credit under criteria established by state medical boards, specialty societies and national professional organizations.

In view of the well-established and increasing use of video for medical and medically related education and continuing education, it would seem that the demand for high quality, professionally produced video materials should increase, providing new opportunities for publishers in the field.

NATURE AND SIZE OF MARKET

Not surprisingly, the dealer, producer and manufacturer perception of the medical segment of the video market is hazy. Medical users constitute an estimated 20% of the total nonbroadcast market and consist mainly of institutions with limited budgets. By and large, these institutions do not require elaborate production facilities, especially when the primary use of television is for student instruction. In a series of telephone interviews conducted by the author, medical users expressed no need for equipment uniquely geared to a medical setting.

Institutional Users

To an extent, the medical market overlaps both the government and education segments. For example, a university with both a medical school and a nursing school would, by one definition, be classified as an educational user. Then, too, a Veterans Administration hospital could be considered either a "government" or a "medical" user. However, the size of the market among uniquely medical institutions is substantial. Table 7.2 lists the number of schools in each of the health professions as well as the total number of hospitals in the United States.

In an attempt to assess the extent of video use among hospitals, the American Hospital Association (AHA) in 1978 conducted a survey of all hospitals in the United States. Based on a response rate of more than 90%, it determined that 50% of all hospitals were equipped with ¾-inch video cassette playback devices while .5% had ½-inch VCR equipment. Of hospitals with 100 beds or less (3800 institutions fit this description), 17%

Table 7.2: Hospitals/Medical Schools in the U.S.

Total hospitals	7271
Schools	
Chiropractic	13
Dentistry	59
Medicine	114
Osteopathy	9
Nursing	1349
Optician	28
Optometry	12
Pharmacy	72
Podiatry	5
Total schools	1661

Source: *Health Resources Statistics,* 1976-77 edition (Washington, DC: Department of Health, Education and Welfare, National Center for Health Statistics, n.d.).

had ¾-inch equipment. A total of 98% of all hospitals reported having 16mm film equipment. The same survey also established that more than 500 hospitals were using closed circuit television for patient education. The AHA did not seek to determine other video uses within hospitals or to establish how many institutions were equipped to produce programming.

A slightly differing estimate of the extent of video use within hospitals was provided by the Network for Continuing Medical Education.[2] NCME agrees that the vast majority of hospitals are equipped with ¾-inch playback devices but notes that based on orders received during 1979 the number of its own subscribers with ½-inch equipment has increased from 3.5% to 10.7%, a trend which is expected to continue. NCME estimates that in the course of a year some 130,000 physicians view one or more of its programs.

Based on the AHA and NCME assessments, it becomes obvious that the 81 medical respondents to the *Video Register* survey (to be discussed later in this chapter) represent only a small fraction of current medical users. It can be assumed that virtually all medical schools and at least half the hospitals in the U.S. are video users, a total of roughly 5000 institutions.

[2]Telephone conversation with the author.

Individual Physician Use

No firm estimates are available as to how many physicians have playback equipment for their personal use in home or office, although a review of warranty cards returned to manufacturers by Tele-Research, Inc., a Warrington, FL distributor of CME programming, indicated that between 8% and 15% of all physicians currently have video cassette players in their homes or offices. If so, the current home market for CME tapes would range from 27,875 to 52,266 physicians.

NCME began to offer programming to individual physicians in 1979 and by the spring of 1980 had 1000 subscribers. It expected to undertake a promotional drive in the spring and summer of 1980 and planned to offer a "movie club" as an inducement to subscribe. The American Medical Association has expressed interest in serving individual physicians, in addition to the local and regional medical associations it currently provides with CME programming.

The Emory Medical Television Network distributes its continuing medical education programs to individual physicians through Tele-Research, which also distributes programs from other producers. In March of 1980 Tele-Research reached an agreement with the Southern Medical Association (SMA) for accreditation of the materials it distributes. At present, Tele-Research distributes programming to "several hundred" individual physicians as well as to small clinics and hospitals with ½-inch playback equipment. Now that Tele-Research programming has been recognized by the SMA, it plans to undertake a direct mail campaign, place advertisements in medical journals and market its materials nationwide through Profesco, Inc., a New York subsidiary of the John Hancock Insurance Co., which has a sales force of 750 in direct contact with individual physicians.

PROSPECTS

The prospects for growth in the medical segment of the nonbroadcast market are particularly promising. The expanding number of applications discussed above provide evidence of the value of television as a communications, treatment and instructional tool in a medical setting.

And, as previously stated, medicine has been remarkably receptive to technological innovation and quick to perceive and implement the various uses to which new and/or existing technology can be put.

It is clear, however, that the increasing emphasis on video in this market is related more to its suitability in everyday applications — student instruction, patient education, public relations, continuing education and staff training — than to more specialized and exotic uses. Of these, continuing professional education and patient education seem most likely to grow as areas of video use.

The proliferation of cable television systems throughout the United States and the readiness of medical institutions to employ cable for continuing education promises wider access to materials presently available and should stimulate increased production. The University of Texas Medical Center at Dallas (see case study) has requested and received approval for a channel when the city's cable franchise is awarded (scheduled for the summer of 1980). While this type of distribution undoubtedly will benefit the medical community, the possibilities for a much wider application are significant. For example, patient education programming (for both in- and out-patients) could be adapted for cable viewing, and a broad range of health education materials might be developed for distribution to the general public. Eventually, with two-way cable systems, viewers might be able to question physicians on television, thereby increasing the public's access to medical care and reducing the time individual physicians and patients must spend on the telephone or in the doctor's office.

At present, however, it must be concluded that the uses of video within the medical segment of the market are not significantly different from those within any of the other market segments. If there is an important difference, it is that video has been enthusiastically and unreservedly accepted as a valuable communications and instructional tool and that this technology-minded market segment is perhaps more imaginative and far-sighted than some of the others in its perception of how widely television can be used.

SURVEY FINDINGS

A total of 81 medical schools and hospitals participated in the *Video Register* survey, representing 7.4% of all respondents. The following is a summary of survey findings for this segment. (Chapter 3 presents data comparing the responses of medical users and other groups to selected survey questions.)

Size of Network

More than 75% of medical respondents had between one and 25 playback locations. Only about 6% had more than 100. (For additional data and comparison with all users, see Table 3.2.)

Uses of Video

Among the medical users video programming was most widely applied to in-service education and continuing education, with about 55% identifying those categories. Nearly half of medical respondents also used video for student instruction and employee training. Actually, there is no clear distinction between these four categories; conversations with many survey respondents indicate that medical institutions often use "in-service education" as an umbrella term embracing student instruction, continuing education and employee training. A category not specified on the questionnaire but frequently mentioned by medical users when asked to list "other" uses was patient education. (For additional data and comparison with all users, see Table 3.3.)

Supervision of Video Services

The media or audiovisual department was most often cited as the entity with administrative authority over video services. (For additional data and comparison with all users, see Table 3.4.) However, some 40% of participants failed to answer this question.

1979 Program Production

Only 3% of the medical users did not report producing their own programs in 1979. Just over 43% produced between 1 and 12 programs, and 54% produced 13 or more; 11% produced 60 or more, or an average of more than 5 per month. (For comparison with all users, see Table 3.5.)

1980 Programming

The vast majority (more than 70%) of medical users expected to increase production in 1980. About 32% expected an increase in off-the-shelf program purchases; 20% expected an increase in rentals. Only a very small percentage anticipated declines in production, purchases or rentals. (For comparison with all users, see Table 3.7.)

Hardware Expenditures

Just under 30% of all medical users valued their video hardware at less than $100,000. Less than 10% reported having $300,000 or more worth of equipment. A substantial number (41.8%) of respondents did not provide this information.

Similarly, nearly half of the respondents did not answer the survey question on funds allocated for new equipment purchases in 1980. Of those responding, only 9% anticipated spending $50,000 or more. (For comparison with all users, see Tables 3.9 and 3.10.)

Video Budgets

The majority of reported total video budgets were in the $10,000-$99,999 range, and 16.5% were $100,000 or larger. (For comparison with all users, see Table 3.12.) Here again, a large number of respondents failed to answer this question.

Other Findings

Equipment and facilities

• Among medical users more than 61% had ¾-inch VTRs, with 42% reporting ½-inch equipment. Slightly under 10% had 1- or 2-inch formats.
• Nearly 70% of respondents had a video studio.
• Three quarters of the medical participants had editing equipment.
• Only a small percentage (6.2%) had the capacity to duplicate 10 or more tapes at a time.
• Most (84%) of the respondents owned cameras; the majority had between one and three. About 73% had studio cameras, 69% had portables; 84% had color, 70% black-and-white.

Personnel

• Some 90% of medical users had full-time video staffs; more than half of these consisted of between one and three persons. About 40% reported having part-time personnel.
• Large video staffs (seven or more), including part-time personnel, were reported by one fourth of medical users.
• Only about one fourth of this group reported hiring additional staff for special projects. (More than half of the survey participants did not answer this question.)
• About two thirds of the medical users did not have a professional video engineer on staff.
• The majority of reported video personnel budgets ranged from $10,000 to $49,999, with the greatest concentration in the $25,000-$49,999

range. (More than 50% did not give information on personnel budgets.)

Programming

• More than 40% of medical respondents reported no off-the-shelf program purchases; of those who did make such purchases, the majority bought fewer than 12 programs in a year-long period.

• Program rentals were even less common, with more than 55% reporting no rentals at all. No users in this category reported renting more than 60 programs per year.

• The vast majority of medical respondents did not seek outside production assistance.

• Fewer than half of these users provided information on per program production costs. Of those who did, about 15% reported a "typical" cost of $2000 or more; about 20% said it was under $600.

Anticipated purchases

• Cameras. New camera purchases were planned by 30% of medical users in 1980; 9% said they planned to spend $10,000 or more on cameras.

• VTRs. Over 34% reported plans to purchase VTRs during the year; 9% indicated a budget of $10,000 or more for VTR purchases.

• Editors. More than 22% anticipated 1980 purchases of editing equipment, with 6% planning to spend $10,000 or more.

• Lights. Planned purchase of lights was indicated by 16% of the medical users.

• Audio equipment. Twenty-four percent of this group said they would purchase audio equipment in 1980.

• Other production equipment. Of all medical respondents, 2% plan to purchase a monitor, 5% a character generator, 5% a time base corrector, 5% a switcher and 2% a special effects generator.

Anticipated budgets

• More than 20% of respondents anticipated a budget increase in 1980, and nearly 24% expected their budgets to continue the upward trend during the next five years. (More than 65% did not respond to the question.)

CASE STUDIES

JOHNS HOPKINS MEDICAL SCHOOL
Division of Audio/Visual Programs
1721 East Madison St.
Baltimore, MD 21205

Johns Hopkins Medical School has an elaborate two-way audio and television system connecting the medical school with outlying medical centers for the instruction of students. The system permits questions to be answered during class and a certain amount of conferencing. In addition to the use of video for classroom instruction, a number of medical departments throughout the hospital itself have their own video equipment. For example, the department of neurosurgery has its own camera controlled by the operating surgeon. All operations are televised to the office of the department head, who can record them if he chooses. Television is also used when there is an overflow audience for a class or lecture so those who cannot get in can view the presentation elsewhere.

Although video is used heavily within the school and the hospital, there is only limited program production. An estimated six to 10 programs are produced each year for in-house viewing only. Film production is more extensive; the school's media library contains 30 film titles produced in-house but only five originally produced video tapes.

The school and hospital have so many playback locations that "no accurate count" is readily available. There is a television studio equipped with six studio and 15 portable cameras, all of them color. There are five full-time staff members.

Despite the heavy reliance on video for both student instruction and documentation, no packaged programs were either purchased or rented from outside sources during the past year.

The total video budget is $204,696 including $84,790 for salaries. New equipment is purchased on an "as needed" basis and is not budgeted in advance. Video production costs range from $150 to $14,000 per program with $600 considered "typical."

KINGSBORO PSYCHIATRIC CENTER
681 Clarkson Ave.
Brooklyn, NY 11203

Kingsboro Psychiatric Center is a New York State facility responsible for all psychiatric services provided by the state in Brooklyn, NY. It provides both in-patient and out-patient services and works in conjunction with other city hospitals as well as with its own clinics located throughout Brooklyn. There are 1300 patients hospitalized at the center for long-term care.

Video is used at Kingsboro for employee training, student instruction, in-service instruction, orientation, continuing education, research and public relations.

The center tapes therapy and interview sessions for use in evaluating a student-trainee's technique in handling patients. Family therapy sessions are also taped occasionally, again for instructional purposes. Most tapes made of individual therapy sessions are erased after they have been reviewed by students and faculty members.

The use of video for research is limited, but occasionally tapes are made of patients before they are placed on medication, and a few months later, so that physicians can observe the side effects of certain psychotropic drugs. A few orientation and training tapes have been produced specifically for new employees and several programs have been made in connection with continuing education requirements of the center's social workers, occupational therapists and rehabilitation therapists.

The center neither purchases nor rents tapes but upon occasion it has filled requests from similar facilities for rentals of its own materials. One production that has generated a number of requests is a compilation of 10 family therapy sessions edited down to a 45-minute tape, which gained attention after it was favorably reviewed in the *Journal of Hospital and Community Psychiatry*.

Kingsboro has been involved with video since 1972. It has a five-camera studio with electronic editing equipment and is staffed by three full-time employees, including a professional video engineer. During 1979, it produced five programs, purchased none and rented four. No change is seen in the rate of production during 1980.

The value of video hardware at the center is placed at $250,000, with another $5000 budgeted for VTR purchases. Production expenditures are minimal, with costs ranging from $10 to $150. A typical program costs only $100 to produce.

The annual video budget amounts to $45,000. It has remained stable since 1978 but is expected to increase by 11% to 15% during the next five years.

PHILADELPHIA COLLEGE OF OSTEOPATHIC MEDICINE
4150 City Line Ave.
Philadelphia, PA 19131

The Philadelphia College of Osteopathic Medicine has an enrollment of

800 students. It is associated with an adjoining 212-bed hospital and uses video for student instruction, patient information and education, public relations, news and information, research, continuing education and in-service education. The principal use, however, is student instruction.

Most programming is designed to teach osteopathic techniques. The format generally includes an introduction by the faculty member teaching the course, who provides a running commentary while techniques are demonstrated. Most programs run between 20 and 30 minutes. They are usually shown in the classroom and laboratory before students actually attempt to practice the technique in question and again afterwards as a review.

The college media department has also produced three patient education programs for transmission over closed circuit television into the hospital rooms of patients about to undergo surgery or specialized tests. One of the programs, on anesthesia, is designed to inform the patient about what can be expected to occur. It provides a behind-the-scenes look at preparations for surgery and the equipment and procedures used in anesthesia.

In addition to classroom showings at the Philadelphia campus, most of the video programs rotate among centers throughout the state where students receive part of their training.

The college has a television studio equipped with four portable and three studio cameras. Five of them are color and two black-and-white. There is also electronic editing equipment. The present video facility has been in operation for five years.

Two full-time and three part-time employees constitute the staff of the media unit. During 1979, a total of 24 programs were produced and this level of production is expected to remain the same for the foreseeable future. The college has purchased some video programming from outside sources. However, as an osteopathic rather than a medical school, it relies for the most part on its own productions, since most available programming is medically oriented. It also makes use of programming provided by pharmaceutical houses which is exhibited with its full commercial content.

The value of the video equipment at the college is estimated at $200,000, with $8000 budgeted for the purchase of additional cameras, $2500 for additional VTRs and $7000 for endoscopic television equipment.

The video facility does not have a separate budget and deems itself "passive" in terms of future production since requests for programming come from faculty members as needs arise. However, plans to relocate the unit in a new campus building late in 1980 may permit an expansion of facilities and production.

SCHOOL OF BASIC MEDICAL SCIENCES
University of Illinois
202 Medical Sciences Building
Urbana, IL 61801

The School of Basic Medical Sciences at Urbana is a sister school of the University of Illinois and Chicago and is part of the University of Illinois School of Medicine system. Each of the four schools within the School of Medicine system has its own television facility, equipment and staff, and each is solely responsible for its own video activity.

At Urbana, video production is directed by the school's media resource manager. There is a small studio, approximately 20 feet by 30 feet, and a 12-foot by 15-foot control room. Equipment includes two Sony 1210 and two 1610 color cameras, as well as two Sony black-and-white cameras. There are nine locations equipped to play back video programming. All but one of the VTRs are ¾-inch machines.

The staff consists of one full-time employee (the media resource manager) and two part-time employees. Occasionally, additional staff is hired for specific productions.

In order of importance, the applications of video at Urbana include: student instruction, documentation and medical research. In addition, video is used for orientation, in-service education and continuing education.

One of the most frequent uses of video for student instruction involves taping students as they interview patients to compile a medical history. The patients are trained to take part in these practice sessions, and the tape is used so that both students and faculty members can evaluate a student's performance. The school also tapes case presentations by students to other students and to a staff physician who is present as a tutor/supervisor. The student making the presentation is required to explain the medical problem, make his or her diagnosis and suggest appropriate treatment. The tapes are later evaluated by the faculty and help to monitor student progress.

The video facility has also produced short tapes for orientation to parents and to other visitors. It has not produced any materials specifically for use in continuing education, but may present a tape from the science library at meetings or continuing education programs held at the school.

Occasionally, video is used in conjunction with medical research programs, primarily to tape the behavior of a research animal over a period of hours for subsequent study by the researcher on the project. In addition, tapes are sometimes made of guest lectures.

The School of Basic Medical Sciences rarely purchases video programming from outside sources, primarily because of limited resources. Not more than 10 tapes per year are acquired from outside sources.

Because the video facility is now five years old, the school plans to begin to replace equipment purchased at the outset. It estimates the total value of the equipment currently in use at approximately $50,000.

UNIVERSITY OF TEXAS, HEALTH SCIENCE CENTER/DALLAS
Department of Biomedical Communications
5323 Harry Hines Blvd.
Dallas, TX 75235

One of four medical schools within the University of Texas, the Health Science Center at Dallas is a teaching hospital and medical school with an enrollment of 500 students. An additional 400 to 500 students are enrolled in the graduate school of health sciences and 300 to 400 more in the affiliated school of allied health. Therefore, the total potential audience for video programming produced by the Department of Biomedical Communications is about 1400 persons.

The department employs 65 persons to work with the faculty in developing instructional material. Twelve of these employees, including a producer/director, video engineer, production assistant and clerical staff, are assigned to the television unit. The unit produces approximately 300 programs per year on a wide range of subjects. Production is done on a recovery basis — that is, the unit charges for its services in order to recover the cost of its supplies and equipment.

Programming is developed by the staff and is heavily oriented to clinical practice. Much of it involves taping student-patient interaction so that the student's performance can be criticized later by a faculty member. There are also more elaborate productions, such as a recent program on genetics for second-year medical students which included animation and a quiz. Most tapes are between 20 and 30 minutes long.

The video unit has also produced some staff training programs for hospital employees. These usually are single-concept programs such as "How to Clean a Catheter."

In an effort to bolster production, the video unit is considering developing its own programming and occasionally does some production work for outside institutions, including two other branches of the University of Texas, the American Heart Association (which is head-quartered in Dallas) and the March of Dimes. It maintains a tape library and keeps a copy of every program produced. When appropriate, it seeks the permission of the client to rent or sell a program to other institutions. However, more than 90% of the programs produced are reserved for internal use only.

Some video programming is purchased for the Health Sciences Center by its Learning Resources Center upon faculty request.

The video unit was established in 1970 with a small, full-color studio and a staff of two. There are now two studios, the main production studio equipped with three color cameras and ¾-inch mastering equipment and a second studio with two cameras. In 1979, approximately 150 programs were produced, and this number is expected to increase in 1980.

The value of hardware totals $700,000 and another $100,000 was budgeted for new cameras in 1979. Production expenditures can range from $150 to $2500, with $500 being "typical." The unit's budget totals $282,500, of which $160,000 is for staff salaries, $20,000 for operations, $100,000 for new equipment and $2500 for travel. The total represents a modest increase over the previous year and is expected to increase by 1% to 5% in 1980. However, over the next five years an 11% to 15% increase in the video budget is anticipated.

8

Nonprofit Organizations

In addition to the major market segments already discussed, smaller categories of users have emerged during the past decade. The largest of these small groups is composed of religious organizations. Other video users not easily classified as business/industry, education, medical or government include libraries, performing arts groups and social service organizations. Together, they compose a market of nonprofit organizations for video applications.

There is some overlap between these institutions and other categories of video users. Libraries, for example, could be considered part of the educational market or, because of their public funding, the government market. Similarly, religious institutions often use video for educational purposes (producing or purchasing programs for parochial schools) and might be viewed as a component of the educational market.

RELIGIOUS INSTITUTIONS

Video applications among religious organizations include continuing education, public service programming and employee communications, in addition to student instruction. (See case study of Pastoral Communications.)

The First Baptist Church of Alcoa, TN, for example, began using video in 1974 to broadcast Sunday services from its main auditorium, but has since expanded its activities to a number of nonbroadcast uses. It has established a video library of programs, religious services and special

125

church productions for loan to individuals with VCRs at home. Many of these tapes are distributed to shut-ins, nursing home patients and others unable to attend regular church services. The church's Video Bible Institute, a series of religious study courses, has given flexibility to religious education programs; students can come to the church to view the programs at their convenience rather than attend scheduled classes. In addition, the church has a closed circuit television system throughout the building, which has allowed it to double its seating capacity for special events such as concerts.

The Church of Latter Day Saints (Mormon) produces religious instructional materials for the deaf on video tape. It is also considering conversion of a number of its films to video. Films and tapes are distributed nationwide from a central facility in Salt Lake City.

Video has also been used by religious groups for recruiting purposes. The Claretians, a Roman Catholic community of priests, has produced a number of programs in an effort to recruit college students to work in its projects in poor areas of the United States and in underdeveloped countries. The programs are on varied subjects of public interest — for instance, a talk on "The Medical Implications of Nuclear Energy" — and include segments explaining the Claretians' service. Programs are distributed to private and public colleges, universities and junior colleges as well as to Catholic institutions.

Video applications among Jewish organizations include fundraising, education, public relations and volunteer training. The Jewish Media Service, a New York-based affiliate of the Council of Jewish Federations and the United Jewish Appeal, is preparing a video catalog for distribution to local and regional Jewish media centers, Jewish community centers, educational institutions and Jewish Federations throughout the country. Programs are selected from institutional media departments and centers, general video programming distributors and overseas sources including Israel. Programs are chosen for their special applicability to the needs of the Jewish community. Many were originally produced for broadcast television.

A major source for Jewish programming is the United Jewish Appeal, which produces a variety of films, television and radio spots, and photograph and slide shows for use during its nationwide fundraising campaigns and for educational and public relations purposes. One video tape describes "Project Renewal," an urban development program in Israel; another is a documentary on the signing of the Israeli-Egyptian peace treaty. The organization also tapes network television newscasts in order to chronicle their presentation of news related to Israel. Some programming has been designed to train volunteers for fundraising campaigns and includes taped role-playing sessions.

LIBRARIES

An estimated 400 to 500 libraries throughout the United States have established video services. Some have concentrated on simply building a collection of prerecorded tapes, following the traditional role of libraries as collectors and repositories of information. Many, however, have become more active video users and produce programming for a variety of applications including staff training, student instruction, public service information, documentation of local events, and services to the handicapped or disadvantaged. Some of these institutions have their own studios and/or equipment, while others rent them.

One of the more notable collections of video tapes is held by the Donnell Library Center, a branch of the New York Public Library. The Donnell's Video Study Center has more than 400 tapes (and 4000 films) acquired from independent producers and video artists. The Center's facilities are also made available to patrons who bring in their own tapes for viewing.

A number of libraries sponsor workshops to train community residents in video production. The Port Washington (NY) Public Library is a leader in this area; community volunteers have produced about 80% of the library's 700-tape video collection, including an oral history collection and tapes of local events and interest. Programs produced by the library staff include taped interviews with artists whose works are on exhibit at the library.

Among libraries that use video for staff training is the Denver Public Library. Training tapes describing library services and procedures serve the library's 22 branches and two bookmobiles. Representative titles include "Service to the Disabled Patron" and "Bad News for Our Books," which explains proper check-out procedures.

Student instruction is one service offered by the video program at the River Bend (IL) Library System. In cooperation with Black Hawk College, River Bend offers a program called Study Unlimited. The college supplies eight courses on video tape; River Bend supplies seven area libraries with video cassette players. As a result, Black Hawk College students may register for courses, buy books, attend videotaped lectures and take finals at their local libraries.

Among video services to the handicapped or disadvantaged are the Deaf Action Program of the Framingham (MA) Public Library and the Video-Mail Program of the Kern County (CA) Library System, which enables shut-ins to review and order books they wish to read.

A number of libraries have become involved with cablecasting via public access channels. The Memphis-Shelby County (TN) Public Library and Information Center, for instance, telecasts children's stories, a series on jazz musicians, city council meetings, interviews with community leaders, and special local events. Its video reference program provides information on library resources.[1]

SOCIAL SERVICE ORGANIZATIONS

Video use by nonprofit social service institutions seems to be less widespread than it is among religious organizations and libraries. The most appropriate video applications for these organizations are those associated with fundraising activities, volunteer motivation, public relations and staff training. Video can also be used to provide access to seminars or conferences for persons unable to attend. It would appear that only fairly large nonprofit organizations, particularly those with regional and branch offices, could afford to establish and maintain a video facility. Among the nonprofit organizations known to use video are United Way of America (see case study), the American Red Cross and Save the Children.

One example of a somewhat smaller service institution that maintains a video facility is the Armenian General Benevolent Union of America (AGBU), headquartered in New York City. Originally established for broadcast purposes, the AGBU's video program has recently been expanded to include nonbroadcast applications in public relations, chapter development and performing and fine arts activities. Video tapes about various AGBU events, services and new programs are produced in New York and forwarded upon request to many of the organization's nationwide chapters for membership viewing, or during new-member campaigns. The AGBU's folk dance ensemble often uses video tapes of rehearsals for work-study purposes. In an effort to cut touring costs, the AGBU drama group videotapes its performances and distributes them to distant chapters whose membership would otherwise be unable to see a production.

PERFORMING ARTS GROUPS

Video can be extremely useful to performing artists, enabling them to record both performances and rehearsals for later study and evaluation.

---

[1]For additional information on the use of video in libraries, see Alice H. Bahr, *Video in Libraries: A Status Report, 1979-80* (White Plains, NY: Knowledge Industry Publications, Inc., 1980).

Dance troupes, in particular, have explored this medium. The Joffrey Ballet, the Murray Louis Dance Company, the Martha Graham Dance Company, the Alwyn Nikolais Company, the New York City Ballet, the Alvin Ailey Dance Company and the Erick Hawkins Dance Company all use video.

Video is a particularly useful tool for dancers because they, more than other performers, have a visual memory and can best recall and repeat movements after seeing them. Thus, a dancer who has not performed a particular ballet in several months may view a tape of a performance as a more efficient means of recalling the choreography than being coached or using dance notation. Then, too, taping a choreographer in the process of rehearsing his or her work with a company can provide a permanent record of the precise details and the emphasis the choreographer intends. Video tapes also give both professionals and the public a means of seeing great dancers after they are no longer actively performing.

Video also is being used to teach dance itself. Fernando Bujones, a dancer with the American Ballet Theatre, has taped a series of half hour video cassette courses on the technique of classical ballet entitled "Fernando Bujones in Class." Individual tapes sell for $100 each.

SURVEY FINDINGS

This segment of the *Video Register* survey consisted of 44 nonprofit, primarily religious, organizations and represented 4% of the total sample. Because of the small number of users included in this group, and the fact that a large percentage of them did not respond to many of the survey questions, the data presented in this chapter give only a rough estimate of video use in this area. It should also be noted that most of the religious respondents' video efforts were educational in nature; e.g., the production of programming for use in parochial schools.

The following is a summary of survey findings for this group. (Chapter 3 presents data comparing the responses of nonprofit users and other groups to selected survey questions.)

Size of Network

More than half of these organizations reported between one and 10 playback locations; about 23% had between 11 and 50. Less than 9% had more than 100. (For additional data and comparison with all users, see Table 3.2.)

Uses of Video

Video was used for public relations purposes by about 45% of this group. Other major applications were in-service education, continuing education, student instruction and employee training. (For additional data and comparison with all users, see Table 3.3.) It should be noted that nearly one third of the nonprofit users failed to answer this question.

Supervision of Video Services

Users most often mentioned the education and personnel/human relations departments as having authority over video services. (For additional data and comparison with all users, see Table 3.4.)

1979 Program Production

A fairly high percentage of this group (16%) reported no in-house productions in 1979. About 32% produced 1-12 programs; 52% produced more than 12; 18% produced 60 or more. (For additional data and comparison with all users, see Table 3.5.)

1980 Programming

Production increases in 1980 were anticipated by 59% of this group. Only about 18% expected to increase off-the-shelf program purchases, and only about 11% expected an increase in program rentals. (For comparison with all users, see Table 3.7.)

Hardware Expenditures

In keeping with the limited budgets of most nonprofit institutions, more than 40% of these users valued their hardware at under $100,000. A high percentage of respondents did not answer the question.

Even fewer respondents provided information on budgets for new equipment. Most of those who did indicated a modest investment—under $20,000. (For comparison with all users, see Tables 3.9 and 3.10.)

Video Budgets

More than 60% of these users failed to answer the question on size of their video budgets. The remainder were almost evenly divided between those reporting budgets of less than $100,000 and those reporting $100,000 or more. (For comparison with all users, see Table 3.12.)

Other Findings

Equipment and facilities

- Half of this group reported using ¾-inch VTRs; about 32% had ½-inch equipment. Less than 5% owned other formats.
- More than 80% of these users had a video studio.
- About 70% owned editing equipment.
- A relatively high percentage (9%) had the capacity to duplicate 10 or more tapes.
- Among these respondents 84% owned cameras. Nearly 48% had studio cameras, about 66% had portables; 59% had color, 48% black-and-white.

Personnel

- More than 88% of this group had full-time video staffs; 52% of them consisted of 1-3 persons. About 52% reported having part-time personnel.
- Large video staffs (seven or more) were reported by about 18% of these respondents.
- About 23% of this group hired additional staff on occasion. (Nearly 60% did not answer this question.)
- More than 61% of this segment did not employ a staff video engineer.
- Only 42% of this group supplied information on video personnel budgets. Of these, the great majority reported budgets of under $100,000, with the greatest concentration falling in the $25,000-$49,999 range.

Programming

- Only 20% of nonprofit users reported off-the-shelf programming purchases.
- Program rentals were reported by 27% of this segment.
- Outside production assistance was sought by a relatively high percentage of these users, with more than 38% reporting such arrangements.
- "Typical" production expenditures were understandably low among these users, with 16% reporting a cost of under $600. About 13% were in the $1000-$1999 range, and less than 7% spent above that amount. (Nearly two thirds of the group did not answer the question.)

Anticipated purchases

- Cameras. More than 25% planned to purchase new cameras in 1980; about 6% anticipated expenditures of $10,000 or more.
- VTRs. Roughly 39% anticipated new VTR purchases; about 6% planned to spend $10,000 or more.
- Editors. About 16% expected to buy editing equipment during the year, with 3% planning to spend $10,000 or more for such purchases.
- Lights. Plans to buy lights were reported by 19% of these respondents.
- Audio equipment. Nearly 23% said they would purchase audio equipment in 1980.
- Other production equipment. Among nonprofit users, 6% reported plans to buy a character generator, 17% a switcher.

Anticipated budgets

- More than half of the nonprofit segment did not answer the question on projected budgets. Of those who did give this information, 29% expected budgets to rise in 1980 and about 42% predicted an increase over a five-year period.

CASE STUDIES

PASTORAL COMMUNICATIONS
Brooklyn Diocese
1712 10th Ave.
Brooklyn, NY 11215

Pastoral Communications is an office within the Diocese of Brooklyn which provides television programming to parochial schools, hospitals and senior citizen centers. It transmits programming via a four-channel, private instructional television fixed service (ITFS) to some 250 schools as well as convents, rectories, monasteries and other diocesan agencies in Brooklyn and Queens, NY. About 180 hours of programming are transmitted each week between the hours of 8 a.m. and 4 p.m. and two nights a week between 7 p.m. and 9:30 p.m.

On a weekly basis, Pastoral Communications provides 42 separate series to elementary schools as well as 18 to 20 programs for high schools and another 18 to 20 for adult education classes. It also maintains a film library from which video tapes are distributed on demand. Pastoral Communications is one of seven such transmission systems in the United States and is working with a consortium of the others to build a satellite interconnection between them. At present, however, its mandate is to provide video services for any agency within the diocese requesting them.

Pastoral Communications began producing its own programs in 1965 and for several years created about 100 programs annually. It suspended most of its own production in the early 1970s when it found packaged programs both cheaper and of higher quality. However, it has recently resumed production of its own materials as part of a broadened effort to provide community service programs of local interest.

The agency produced 50 programs in 1979 and expects in-house production to accelerate. Among recent tapes were a history of the papacy for use during the visit of Pope John Paul II in the fall of 1979, a program designed to explain medical benefits to diocese employees, and a nutrition program to teach various ethnic groups how to compensate in meal planning for national differences in eating patterns.

An effort is being made to provide local hospitals with patient information programs and to address community issues. One program per month is transmitted to senior citizen clubs. It is partly entertainment and partly educational-informational in nature with a question and answer period (questions are telephoned to the studio).

For elementary students, the agency has produced an educational game for use in teaching the scriptures. High school level programs have treated subjects ranging from narcotics to the sciences, literature, guidance and counseling issues as well as religious subjects. For adults in high school equivalency courses, programs have concerned the scriptures, parenting and specific topics such as how to deal with teenagers with drug problems.

Pastoral Communications has a studio at its Brooklyn headquarters equipped with six black-and-white cameras, five of them studio cameras and one portable. There is a staff of 20 full-time and two part-time employees. Additional help is hired as needed and there is a professional video engineer on staff.

Specific budget information is not available for publication, but the agency has plans to convert to color and to purchase recorders, character generators, editors and time-base correctors.

UNITED WAY OF AMERICA
801 North Fairfax St.
Alexandria, VA 23314

United Way of America is a nonprofit organization that serves as a national spokesman for a major segment of the voluntary sector. It is an umbrella organization for some 2300 local United Ways throughout the United States. These local groups conduct fundraising campaigns and distribute contributions to qualified voluntary agencies on the local level.

For the past two years the national organization has been using video as a means of communication with the local organizations, for public relations, for promotional purposes during fundraising campaigns and as a training device to help officials on the local level prepare themselves for television appearances in connection with their fundraising activities.

The national organization tapes speeches at its annual convention and makes them available on ¾-inch cassettes to local representatives who were present and to those who were unable to attend. It has also produced and distributed promotional materials to the local organizations as an aid in their fundraising. And although it does not produce any regularly scheduled video programming for use in the field, it has made available a half-hour show titled "Video Potential" to local organizations in 65 cities as a test of this means of presenting information and conducting training activities.

Video also has been used as a means of presenting and reviewing management issues that occur at both the local and national level. The national organization produced a 10-minute video segment designed for use in a three-hour program produced by the National Academy for Volunteerism to help nonprofit organizations make better use of their boards of directors.

A drawback to United Way's video effort is the lack of playback facilities at the local level. Although there are 2300 individual United Ways throughout the country, many are in very small communities and only 35 of them have their own playback units. A total of 1100 copies are made of all productions but most recipients must borrow equipment in order to view them.

The national organization describes its video facilities as "modest." There is a studio equipped with six cameras and editing equipment. Nevertheless, most editing as well as all duplication are handled by outside production service companies. There is a staff of two full-time and one part-time employees.

United Way plans to upgrade its production facilities and enlarge its studio but considers this a long-term project that may take up to 10 years to complete. It budgeted $18,000 for new equipment in 1979 and planned to spend approximately half of that on new VTRs and the remainder on production equipment including a vectorscope and SMPTE time code generating and display equipment. It is considering a switch in format to ½-inch video cassettes.

An average of $5000 is spent on each United Way production, a figure that does not include staff salaries. The total video budget for the 1979 fiscal year was $83,000, of which $48,000 was earmarked for staff salaries.

9

Summary and Outlook

The 1980s should be another decade of growth for the nonbroadcast video market. This growth will take place in three areas: new applications, new technology and new users.

NEW APPLICATIONS

Once an organization has adopted video, it will tend to find an increasing number of uses for the medium. When the distribution system is in place, people become accustomed to the idea of using video as a means of communication in their working or studying environments, not just as an entertainment medium in their homes. Management learns to consider video as one alternative approach to a problem or new project. For example, where the first video venture may have been a program on employee benefits, the firm may soon be regularly producing informative programs on new products, changes in management policy, etc.

Many of these "new" applications are simply new to the organization and are not innovative in nature, although there will be different approaches to the same type of programming. There are numerous "small" users of video now who should be expanding their video operations in this way over the next decade. However, a few relatively new areas of video programming should gain increasing acceptance in the next few years.

In the business/industry sector video is being used to boost employee morale, for example, and to tape role-playing sessions in sales training programs. Other newer applications include programming aimed at audiences other than company employees. These include point-of-sale display tapes; programs used by salespeople to present new products to potential customers; and programs on how to operate equipment or office products that can be used by or instead of market support personnel. Some firms are also using video for recruiting, public relations and, occasionally, the entertainment of customers.

In the field of medicine, an exciting possibility for the use of video is for remote diagnosis, consultation and patient examination. Although only a few demonstrations of telemedicine have occurred, this application could make quality medical care accessible to even the most distant locations, and sharply reduce the time and costs expended on specialists' consultations. However, it is unlikely that telemedicine will be used extensively in the near future. A growing area of medical programming is that for patient education. Video used to explain a medical procedure or demonstrate treatment, for example, can be much more effective than verbal or written explanations and can save valuable physician and nurse time. This application should gain widespread acceptance in the next few years.

Educators are using video not only for instruction but increasingly for students' own productions. At the school level, where packaged programming is more prevalent — although still limited — there is great potential for video use, particularly in combination with computers for interactive learning. However, limited budgets and teacher resistance should continue to restrict growth in video at this level. In higher education, on the other hand, there is likely to be wider use of video to present lecture courses, laboratory demonstrations and continuing education material. Institutions should also continue to use video for public relations and recruiting, career training and orientation of both students and faculty.

Notable new and growing uses of video in government include the taping of testimony and depositions to be presented in court, documentation of evidence in crime and fire investigations, and public information/education programming. Numerous training applications, including simulations and documentation of events for personnel evaluation, should also continue to increase.

NEW TECHNOLOGY

One of the major technological developments affecting the market has been the introduction of video disc systems. Video disc technology offers the advantages of easy storage and retrieval, better sound and picture quality, and eventually lower-priced hardware and software — features that could have a profound impact on video use. However, the format is as yet incapable of recording; it can only play back prerecorded programs. Another unresolved problem is that three different and incompatible types of video disc systems have been developed. Programming is being developed for each, but as of 1980 little original software had been created.

Once there is sufficient programming available, video discs should offer particular appeal to educational users. Discs can be used interactively; that is, they are programmed to stop and wait for a response before continuing. A student can therefore work independently at his or her own pace.

This same feature has already made the disc popular for training in companies that have made an early commitment to the new format. Training applications for discs should multiply in all segments of video users over the next decade. In education, it is unlikely that video discs will be widely adopted at the elementary and high school levels for the same reasons that video tape has not been overwhelmingly accepted. Colleges and universities, however, should prove a good market for discs.

Many video disc applications are likely to use the disc in conjunction with other technology, especially the computer. Computer control will facilitate random access to any frame on the disc. It will also manage the interactive applications where the next step in a program is dependent on the response to the previous one.

An important trend in video technology is towards miniaturization. The development of the tiny charge-coupled device (CCD), which is a solid-state substitute for a camera tube, has facilitated the development of much smaller cameras. Good quality, portable color cameras are now available to even small users and use of the CCD should yield even smaller, lightweight cameras.

In-camera recording may be the next advance. Sony has recently announced that it will use a tiny, CCD camera in combination with a small video recorder to produce a single-unit "Video Movie." Although this will not be commercially available until 1985, it is likely that other manufacturers will also produce single unit systems. The Sony product weighs only 4.4 pounds and reportedly will be priced at under $1000, a size and price that should offer immediate appeal to small video users.

Another developing video format that will offer smaller, lighter-weight equipment at a lower price is the longitudinal video recorder (LVR). The LVR system is also a video tape format that uses a fixed video head to scan small multiple-track tape. Such a system requires fewer moving parts, so is small, portable and easy to use.

While small, easy-to-use systems are likely to attract thousands of smaller organizations to the new use of video, larger organizations, often with long-established video networks, should continue to acquire more sophisticated technology. While this will often mean moving to broadcast-quality video tape equipment, it should also include the addition of video disc systems for many training and sales/marketing applications. These larger, usually corporate, users may also turn to other delivery systems, such as cable and satellite. Video teleconferencing using satellite transmission should become a viable alternative for such users.

Still another technology that may spur increased video use in the coming decade is videotext, sometimes known as teletext in its broadcast version and viewdata in its computer-stored version.* In videotext systems, words, numbers and rudimentary graphics are transmitted to the home TV set using special data-encoding techniques; the messages are either sent in unused lines of the broadcast TV signal, or else stored in a computer and retrieved over phone lines or by a two-way cable TV hookup. While videotext systems are operating in Britain, France, Germany, other European countries and Australia, in 1980 they were still undergoing preliminary technical tests in the United States. The technology seems ideally suited for institutional communications, since a company could store information on its prices and products in a computer that would be accessible through a toll-free call by its customers. Latest technical details and prices, available as printed words on the TV screen, could then be supplemented by programming in full motion, color and sound, from an accompanying video tape or disc.

NEW USERS

Most of the new users in the next few years will come from the business and industry sector, although there should be some growth in both medicine and government. As discussed earlier, few new school systems will have the money, even if they have the inclination, to invest in video. Most colleges and universities are already using video, so there is little room for a swelling in numbers there. Within business and industry, there should be particular growth in the service industries, especially wholesalers, retailers and banks. There should also be continued growth in the number of manufacturers and utilities using video.

Many of the new users will be medium-sized organizations that will no longer find costs of video equipment and programming prohibitive, particularly in the face of continuing increases in energy costs. Table 9.1 compares the Consumer Price Index (CPI) figures and VTR prices for 1972 and 1980. As indicated, while the CPI for transportation rose by 108% between 1972 and 1980, the list price of comparable models of a Sony ¾-inch video recorder/player increased only half as much. There are, of

---

*See *Videotext: The Coming Revolution in Home/Office Information Retrieval,* Efrem Sigel, ed. (White Plains, NY: Knowledge Industry Publications, Inc., 1980). This book traces the development of videotext systems around the world and analyzes the outlook for future applications.

course, other costs involved in using video, most notably salaries. However, when substituting a video program for an in-person presentation saves both travel costs and personnel time, the implication is clear that video can be an economical as well as effective communications medium.

Table 9.1. Price Trends, 1972-80

	1972	May 1980	Percent Increase
CPI, all items (1967=100)	125.3	244.9	95.5%
CPI, transportation	119.9	249.0	107.7
List price, ¾-inch VTR:			
playback only[1]	$1100	$1775	61.4
recorder/player[2]	1395	2150	54.1

[1] 1972 price for Sony model VP1100; 1980 price for Sony model VP2010.
[2] 1972 price for Sony model VO1100; 1980 price for Sony model VO2610.
Sources: U.S. Bureau of Labor Statistics; Sony Corp. of America.

A WORD OF CAUTION

Although prospects are good for continued growth in the nonbroadcast video market, there are also inherent difficulties in video use that must be acknowledged. Many new users approach video production with very little, if any, technical knowledge. The temptation to "jump on the bandwagon," and in some cases to "keep up with the Joneses" — competitors who are already involved in video—has led some users to overextend themselves. They have purchased equipment that no one has been trained to operate, resulting in a high level of frustration and possibly in failure to meet programming objectives. In some cases, video was not the best alternative to meet the communications goal. In others, a packaged program would have sufficed. Some users may have been put off by the apparent costliness of customized programming, not realizing that in the long run it might have been cheaper than the costs incurred for overhead, salaries and out-of-pocket expenses, not to mention purchase of the equipment itself.

Even experienced users must consider the fact that a capital investment in equipment that is under-utilized is probably not worth the cost of capital, particularly in a tight-money period. If video program production is irregular, it might be cheaper to rent equipment than to purchase it. Another consideration is that rapidly evolving technology renders video equipment obsolete in a relatively short period of time. Many users might do better to rent equipment at first to test its feasibility and effectiveness in their organizations, and later purchase what they know they need, probably also gaining additional features at a lower price.

As mentioned previously, established users often "step up" to better quality equipment. Some corporate users do so simply to keep up with the state of the art, always to have the latest feature or to use the newest format regardless of the fact that the hardware on hand is more than adequate to meet the organization's video needs. Some of these organizations are actively sought out by the equipment manufacturers (see Chapter 4) who want to create a market for their new products. This trend should help keep equipment sales healthy, but is not always beneficial to the user.

Institutional users often face problems with programming concepts. Since program ideas are often developed by managers with little video expertise, the result may fall short of expectations. In some cases, the emphasis on delivering a message may preclude a creative approach. On the other hand, more elaborate operations with separate video staffs may excel creatively and technically, but may not communicate the intended message clearly. Conflicts can arise as to which is more effective, a straightforward presentation of content or a more creative and technically sophisticated production.

The whole question of effectiveness is one that any present or potential user of video must consider. Unfortunately, it is often difficult to measure the effectiveness of a particular program. Some of the benefits to be gained from certain types of programming are intangible, such as improved employee or patient morale, as opposed to more easily quantified results such as improved student test scores or fewer rejects from quality control. Whether or not direct results can be seen from a video program, effectiveness is a key consideration when an organization is judging the feasibility of a video program, one which some users have ignored.

OUTLOOK

Despite the problems, more and more organizations are making a commitment to video. Not only are they using video, but the majority are producing their own programs. This trend is likely to continue for several reasons. One is that the packaged programming available is limited to generic types that can be used by many organizations, whereas each organization has unique needs dictating the content of a particular video program. As video is increasingly recognized as an important communications tool, rather than just another audiovisual aid, applications will expand and the need for customized programming will grow. Further, it is likely that an organization using video frequently will eventually become involved in doing its own programming rather than contracting with someone outside. This will occur in part to cut costs and in part because of the sheer appeal of technology and a need to keep up with current trends.

An involvement in video entails an often heavy investment in hardware and continuing expenditures for personnel, overhead and out-of-pocket expenses for each program produced. There is also a trend of constant "stepping up" to additional and more complex equipment. Faced with an audience that will not forever tolerate amateurish presentations, organizations continually strive for more sophisticated productions that rival professional programming in quality.

New developments in video technology may find a ready market among established users who are already convinced of the benefits of video. In addition, such developments, which should yield less expensive, easy-to-use equipment, are likely to attract new users.

Even at a rate of growth of 14%, scarcely higher than that of inflation, users' expenditures on video equipment and programming will have nearly doubled by 1985, reaching $2.1 billion. It would not be unreasonable to project a growth rate of 20%, which would yield total expenditures of $2.7 billion by that year.

About the Authors

Paula Dranov is a free-lance journalist and the author of several studies in the communications field, including *Publishing/Programming Opportunities in Consumer Video* and *Inside the Music Publishing Industry.* A graduate of Pennsylvania State University, she has worked for United Press International and the Newhouse News Service as editor and reporter. She is the author of magazine articles on a wide variety of subjects.

Louise Moore is director of research and senior editor of K.I.P. studies for Knowledge Industry Publications. Among the studies she has edited are *The Business Information Markets, 1979-1984* and *Consumer Magazines in the 1980s.* She holds a B.A. from Dickinson College and an M.B.A. from Iona College, and has a background in marketing.

Adrienne Hickey, associate editor of books, monographs and studies for Knowledge Industry Publications, is a graduate of Cornell University. She has worked as an editor for Macmillan Publishing Co. and The Conference Board and as a staff writer for an executive consulting firm.

Appendix A
The *Video Register* Survey

1) Organization Name _____ Ext. _____

           Address _____

_____

    Phone Number _____

  Location of video facility:

_____

_____

    Phone _____ Ext. _____

2) Check the best description of your parent organization:

      _____Business   _____Teaching hospital/Medical school

      _____School/College   _____Government

      _____Other _____

3) Individual responsible for video production activity at this location:

  Name: _____ Title _____

4) How many locations within your organization are equipped to play back programs? _____

  Please categorize by types of equipment:

  ¾ inch Number of machines_____

  ½ inch Number of machines_____

  Other Number of machines_____(please specify)_____

5) Is there a studio at your location?

      _____Yes   _____No

6) How many cameras are there at your location? Total Number_____

  Number of studio_____ Number of color _____

  Number of portable _____Number of b/w _____

7) Do you have electronic editing equipment at your location?

      _____Yes   _____No

8) Are you equipped to duplicate 10 or more tapes at a time "in house" ?

      _____Yes   _____No

9) How many people are associated with the video staff at your location?
Number of full-time _____   Part-time _____
Any additional staff hired for specific productions? _____

10) Is there a professional video engineer on the staff at your location? _____

11) How many programs have you produced at your location in the last 12 months?
_____ In the next 12 months, do you expect this number to:
_____ Increase   _____ Decrease   _____ Remain the same

12) How many packaged programs have you purchased from outside sources in the
last 12 months? _____ In the next 12 months, do you expect this number to:
_____ Increase   _____ Decrease   _____ Remain the same

13) How many packaged programs have you rented from outside sources in the last
12 months? _____ In the next 12 months, do you expect this number to:
_____ Increase   _____ Decrease   _____ Remain the same

14) Do you contract with outside production service companies to produce
programs for your organization?
_____ Yes   _____ No

15) How many other locations within your organization produce or create
programming? _____

16) How many people are associated with the video staffs at other locations? _____

17) If your organization qualifies for listing in another section of THE VIDEO
REGISTER, please check the category below and we will forward the appro-
priate questionnaire:
_____ Manufacturers (of video equipment)
_____ Production and Post-production Services (video)
_____ Dealers (video companies)
_____ Publishers/Distributors (of video programming)

(Questionnaire continues on next page)

The following information is strictly confidential and will NOT appear in THE VIDEO REGISTER: it is being compiled for internal use. If this section is completed, your organization will automatically qualify for a free copy of THE VIDEO REGISTER.

For which of the following does your organization use video? (check all that apply)

_____ Employee training	_____ Orientation
_____ Sales and marketing	_____ Documentation
_____ Public relations	_____ Safety instruction
_____ Management information	_____ Student instruction
_____ Shareholder information	_____ In-service education
_____ News and information	_____ Research
_____ Entertainment	_____ Continuing education
_____ Other (please specify) _____	

To what department does the video facility report?

_____ Communications	_____ Public Relations
_____ Personnel/Human Resources	_____ Media or A/V
_____ Sales Promotion	_____ Public Affairs
_____ Training	_____ Marketing
_____ Education	
_____ Other (please specify) _____	

What is the value of the hardware currently at your location ? $ _____

How much have you budgeted for total new equipment purchases this year? $_____

Do you plan to purchase any of the following in the next 12 months?

	Estimated budget:
_____ Cameras	$_____
_____ VTRs	$_____
_____ Editing equipment	$_____
_____ Other production equipment (please specify)	
_____	$_____
_____	$_____
_____ Lights	$_____
_____ Audio equipment	$_____
_____ Other _____	$_____

What is your typical expenditure on a video production? $ _____
Minimum expenditure $_____   Maximum expenditure $_____
These figures_____include_____do not include the salaries of staff people.

What is your annual video budget? $_____

What is your total video budget for this fiscal year? $_____

Compared to last year, did your video budget: _____ Remain the same

_____Increase: by 1-5%_____ 6-10%_____ 11-15%_____ 16% or more_____ (_____%)

_____Decrease: by 1-5%_____ 6-10%_____ 11-15%_____ 16% or more_____ (_____%)

Will your budget for the next fiscal year: _____ Remain the same

_____Increase: by 1-5%_____ 6-10%_____ 11-15%_____ 16% or more_____ (_____%)

_____Decrease: by 1-5%_____ 6-10%_____ 11-15%_____ 16% or more_____ (_____%)

Over the next five years, will your budget: _____ Remain the same

_____Increase: by 1-5%_____ 6-10%_____ 11-15%_____ 16% or more_____ (_____%)

_____Decrease: by 1-5%_____ 6-10%_____ 11-15%_____ 16% or more_____ (_____%)

Appendix B

Known Video Users

The following organizations are listed in the 1979-80 edition of *The Video Register*. (The 1980-81 edition, with additional listings and more complete information, will be available from Knowledge Industry Publications in the fall of 1980.)

AC Sparkplug
AMF Hatteras Yachts
AM International
AMP Special Industries
APA Transport Corporation
ARA Services, Inc.
ARCO Oil & Gas Company
AT&T Long Lines (Headquarters)
AT&T Long Lines/Chicago, IL
AT&T Long Lines/Cincinnati, OH
AT&T Long Lines/Washington, DC
AT&T New Jersey
AT&T New York
AT&T Television Studio
Abington Memorial Hospital
Abbott Laboratories
Abilene Christian University, TX
Abraham & Strauss
Acacia Mutual Life
Act Media Services
Acts, Inc.
Adolph Coors Company
Advanced Micro Devices
Advanced Systems Inc.
Advanced Video Products
Aerospace Audiovisual Service
Aetna Life & Casualty
Agape Ministries
Agency for Instructional Television
Aid Association for Lutherans

Aid Insurance Service
Air Canada
Air Products & Chemicals, Inc.
Airco Welding Products
Airwick Industries
Alabama ETV Commission
Alabama Power Co.
The Alaska Christian Television Services
Alcan Aluminum Corporation
Alderson-Broaddus College
Allegheny College
Allen Bradley Company
Allied Chemical Corporation
Allis-Chalmers Corporation
Allstate Insurance Company, Inc.
B. Altman & Co.
Aluminum Company of America
Amarillo College
Ambulatory Care Center
American Airlines A/V Center
American Baptist Churches USA
American Can Company
The American College
American Express
American Family Insurance
American Greetings
American Hospital Association
American Management Associations
American Medical Association
American Motors Corporation
American Mutual Insurance Company

American Red Cross
The American University
Ames, Div. of Miles Laboratories
Ami Ron Productions
Anchorage School District
Anoka-Ramsey Community
  College
The Ansul Company
Appalachian State University
Applied Materials, Inc.
Applied Science Associates
Arapahoe Community College
Archdiocese of New York
  Instructional Television
Arista Records
Arizona Department of Public
  Safety
Arizona State University
Arkansas Technical University
Arlington Public Schools
Arlington School District
Armco, Inc.
Armstrong Cork Company
Arthur Andersen & Company
Arthur Young & Company
Artificial Lift Efficiency School
Ashland Oil, Inc.
Atlanta Interfaith Broadcasters
Auburn University
Aultman Hospital
Aurora Public Schools
Austin Independent School
  District
Automatic Data Processing
Avis Rent-A-Car System, Inc.

B.P. Canada, Ltd.
Babcock & Wilcox
Ball Memorial Hospital
Ball State University
Baltimore City Police Dept.
Bambergers
Bancohio Ohio National Bank
Bank of America
Bankers Life & Casualty Co.
Baptist Medical Center

Baptist Medical Centers
Baptist Memorial Hospital
Barber-Colman Co.
Barkers
Baxter Travenol Laboratories,
  Inc.
Bay Area Community College
  Television Consortium
Baylor College of Medicine
Baylor University
Beach Channel High School
Beatrice Foods Company
Bechtel Video Programming
Beckman Instruments
Bedford Central School District
Bell & Howell
Bell Fibre Products Corporation
Bell System Center for Technical
  Education (AT&T)
Bell Telephone Company of
  Pennsylvania
Bell Telephone Laboratories, Inc.
Bell Telephone Laboratories,
  Inc./Illinois
Bell Telephone Laboratories, Inc.
  /New Jersey
Bendix Kansas City
Bendix Corporation
Bendix Field Engineering
Benet Academy
Bergen Brunswig Corporation
Bergen Community College
Berlin High School
Beth Israel Hospital
Bethlehem Steel Corporation
Big Dog Video
Billikopf Learning Resource
  Center
Bird Machine Company
Black Hawk College
Blackhawk Technical Institute
Bloomingdale's Inc.
Bloomington Video Center
Blythedale Children's Hospital
Boces of Erie & Cattaraugus Dis.
  #2

Boces of Herkimer County
Boces of Hamilton, Fulton,
Montgomery
Boces of Nassau County
Boces of St. Lawrence-Lewis
County
Boces of Saratoga County
Boces of Steuben-Allegany
Boces of Tompkins-Seneca-Tioga
Boeing Aerospace Company
Borg-Warner (York Division)
Boston Catholic Television
Center
Boston College Television
Boston Edison Company
Boston University
Bradley University
Brandeis Department Stores
Bridgewater Town Police
Department
Brigham Young University
The Broadway
Brooklyn College Television
The Brooklyn Museum
Broward Community College
Central Campus
Brown Group, Inc.
Brunswick Corporation
Bucks County Community
College
Buena Vista College
Bullock's
Bur Oak Library Systems
Burdine's
Burke & Company
Burlington County College
Burlington Industries, Inc.
Burroughs Corp.
Butler County Community
College

CBS, Inc.
CBS Broadcast Center, Inc.
CBS Studio Center
CBS Television City
CBS Washington

CCTV Crestwood Community
Television
C&P Telephone
The Cablesystem
John C. Calhoun State
Community College
California College of Podiatric
Medicine & Hospital
California CPA Foundation
California Department of Trans-
portation, District 4
California State Polytechnic
University-Pomona
California State University/
Chico
California State University/
Fullerton
California State University/
Long Beach
California State University/
Northridge
California State University/
Sacramento
Calumet College Communications
Center
Capital District Psychiatric Center
Carnegie Mellon University
Carolina Power & Light Company
Carson Pirie Scott Company
Carvel Corporation
J.I. Case Agricultural Equipment
Division
Case Western Reserve University
Caterpillar Tractor Company
Service Training
Catholic Television Network
Catholic Television Network/
Brooklyn
Catholic TV Network of Chicago
Catholic Television Network of
San Francisco
Cayuga County Community
College
Central Connecticut State College
Central Michigan University
Central Soya Company, Inc.

Central Telephone & Utilities
Central Texas College (KNCT)
Central Washington University
Cerro Coso Community College
Chadron State College
Channel 24 (Local Government Access)
Charles County Community College
Charles Stark Draper Laboratory, Inc.
Chase Manhattan Bank
Chemical Bank
Chesebrough Ponds
Chevrolet Motor Div.
Chestnut Hill College
Chicago Board of Education-Wachborne Trade School
Chicago Bridge & Iron Company
Chicago State University
Chicago Transit Authority
The Children's Hospital
Children's Hospital Medical Center of Akron
Christian Church
Chrysler Corporation
Chubb & Son, Inc.
Ciba-Geigy Corporation
Cine Magnetics Film & Video
Cinekyd Enterprises
Citibank
City University of New York SETV-S.A.M.E.
City University of New York/ York College
Clarion State College School of Communications
Clark Equipment
Clarkson Hospital, Educational Services
Clemente High School
Cleveland Clinic Foundation
Cleveland State University
Climax Molybdenum Co.
Coaxial Communications Company

Colgate Palmolive
College of the Desert
College of Dupage
College of Notre Dame
College of Osteopathic Medicine & Surgery
College of Our Lady of the Elms
College of Physicians & Surgeons
College of Saint Thomas
College of San Mateo (KCSM)
The College of Staten Island
Colonial School District
Color Video Recording Service, Inc.
Colorado State University
Columbia University
Columbus and Franklin County Library System
Columbus, City of, Div. of Police
Columbus Technical Institute
Combined Insurance Company of America
Combustion Engineering, Inc.
Commercial Union Assurance Co.
Communications Concepts International, Inc.
Community College of Allegheny County
Community Hospital of Roanoke Valley
Community Video Services
Concordia College (MN)
Concordia College (OR)
Concordia Teachers College
Connecticut Department of Children and Youth Services
Connecticut General Life Insurance Company
Connecticut Justice Academy
Connecticut Mutual Life Insurance Company
Consolidated Business Systems
Consolidated Edison
Consumers Power Company
The Continental Group, Inc.
Continental Telephone Corp.

Cooperative Extension Service
Cornell University
Corning Glass Works
Corporation for Public
  Broadcasting
Correction Officers Training
  Academy
Cosumnes River College
Council Rock High School
County College of Morris
Cramer Electronics Inc.
Crown Zellerbach Film Lab
Crum & Forster Insurance
The Culinary Institute of
  America
Cuyahoga Community College
Cuyahoga County Office of
  Manpower Development

Dakota Wesleyan University
Dallas Area Hospital TV System
  (DAHTS)
Dallas/Fort Worth Airport
  D.P.S.
Danbury Public Library
Danville School District #18
Dargan-Carver Library
Dartmouth College
Dawson College
Dayco Corporation
Daytona Beach Community
  College
Dayton's
Deaf Missions
Dean Witter Reynolds Inc.
Deere & Company
Defense Information School
DeKalb School System
Delaware County Community
  College
Delaware County Court House
Delaware Technical &
  Community College
Delgado College
Deloitte, Haskins & Sells
Delta College

DePaul Rehabilitation Hospital
Digital Equipment Company
Dillingham Corportion
Diocesan Communications Center
Diocesan Television Center
Diocese of Madison
Diocese of Rockville Center
Dodge City Community College
Doehler-Jarvis Castings
The Dow Chemical Company
Dow Chemical Company-Texas
  Division
Doyle, Dane, Bernbach Inc.
Drake University
Dresser Industries-O.P.G.
Drew University
Dubuque Metropolitan System
Duluth Public Schools
Dundalk Community College
E.I. DuPont de Nemours &
  Company, Inc.
Duquesne University

Ear Research Institute
East Carolina University School
  of Medicine
East Tennessee State University
East Texas State University
Eastern Airlines, Inc.
Eastern Baptist Theological
  Seminary
Eastern Connecticut State
  University
Eastern Illinois University
Eastern Washington University
Eaton Corporation
Eckanar
Economics Laboratory, Inc.
Edison State Community College
Edit/Chicago, Inc.
Edmonds Community College
Educational Productions, Inc.
Educational Television Center
Educational Testing Service
El Paso Community College
Elgin High School

Eli Lilly & Company
Emma Willard School
Emory Medical Television
  Network
Emory University School of
  Dentistry
Employers Insurance of Wausau
Episcopal Church Center
Equifax Inc.
Equitable Life Assurance
  Society
Erie Savings Bank
Eros Data Center
Essex County College
Evans Products Company
Evanston Hospital
Evanston Township High School
Executone, Inc.
Exide Company
Exxon Research & Engineering
Exxon Corporation
Exxon International Inc.

F&R Lazarus
Factory Mutual Engineering
  Corporation
Fairchild Industries
Fairchild Test Systems
Fairleigh Dickinson
Fairview General Hospital
Faso Tragrupac
Fayetteville State University
Federal Correction Institution
  (WI)
Federal Correctional Institution
  (FL)
Federal Emergency Management
  Agency
Federal Intermediate Credit
  Bank
Federal National Mortgage
  Association
Federal Prison System
Federation of Independent Illinois
  Colleges
Felician College

Ferris State College
Fiat-Allis Construction
  Machinery
The Fidelity Bank
Firemen's Fund Insurance
  Companies
Firestone Tire and Rubber
  Company
First National Bank of Chicago
Fisher Scientific Company
Florida Baptist Convention
Florida Department of Education
Florida International University
Florida Power Corporation
Florida Power & Light Company
Florida State University
Florida Technological University
Fluor Television
Foley's
Forbes Health System
Ford Aerospace & Communi-
  cations Corp.
Henry Ford Community College
Ford Motor Company
Fort Worth Police Department
Four Phase Systems, Inc.
The Foxboro Company
Franciscan High School
Frederick Community College
Freightliner Corporation
Furnas Electric Company
Futurevision Cable Enterprises,
  Inc.

GMC Truck & Coach Division
GTE
GTE Automatic Electric, Inc.
GTE Data Services
Gallery of Homes, Inc.
Gateway High School (APS)
Gateway Technical Institute
Geico
Generac Corporation
General Dynamics
General Electric Company
General Health Services

General Mills, Inc.
General Motors Photographic
General Telephone Company of
California
General Telephone Company of
Florida
General Telephone Company of
Illinois
General Telephone Company of
the Northwest
General Telephone Company of
Ohio
General Telephone Company of
the Southeast
General Telephone Company of
the Southwest
General Tire & Rubber Co.
Genrad, Inc.
Geode Productions, Inc.
George Fox College
Georgetown University Family
Center
Georgetown University Medical
Center
Georgia Institute of Technology
Georgia Power Company
Gibbs & Hill
Gimbels
Gimbels Midwest
Gimbels Philadelphia
Gimbels Pittsburgh
Glendale Community College
Glendale Federal Savings
Glendale Unified School District
Golub Corporation
B.F. Goodrich Company
The Goodyear Tire & Rubber
Company
Gould Inc.
Grass-Roots Television
Greater Cincinnati TV
Educational Foundation
Greater Cleveland Hospital
Association
Greater Latrobe School District
Greenburgh Eleven UFSD

Greenwich High School
Television
Gulf Coast JuniorCollege
Gulf Oil Canada, Ltd.
Gulf Oil Corporation
Gustavus Adolphus College

Hahneman Medical College and
Hospital
Half Hollow Hills H.S. East
Halliburton Services
Hamline University
Hampshire College
Hampton Institute
John Hancock Mutual Life
The Handyman of California, Inc.
Harlyn School
William Rainey Harper College
Harrington Memorial Hospital
Harris Data Communications
Harrisburg Area Community
College
Hartford Hospital
The Hartford Insurance Group
Harvard Graduate School of
Education
Harvard Law School
Harvard School of Dental
Medicine
Harvard School of Public Health
Harvard University
Haverhill Public Library
Hawthorne High A.V.A.
Hazelwood School District
Heilig-Meyers Company
Helen Fuld School of Nursing-
West Jersey Hospital
Hempstead Public Schools
Hendrick Medical Center
Hennepin Technical Center
Hercules, Inc.
The Hertz Corporation
Hewlett High School
(WGWH-TV)
Hewlett-Packard Company
Hickory City Schools TV Center

The Higbee Company
Highland Community College
Hinsdale Associates
Hinsdale Sanitarium & Hospital
Hoechst-Roussel Pharma-
    ceuticals, Inc.
Hoffman-LaRoche Inc.
Holiday Inn Executive Con-
    ference Center
Holy Cross Hospital
Honeywell, Inc.
Honeywell, Inc. DSD
Honeywell Information Systems,
    Inc.
Hospital Corporation of America
Houston Police Department
Howard Career Center
Howard University School of
    Communications
HUD Training Center
Hughes Aircraft Company
Hughes Tools Company
Humacao University College
Hurley Medical Center
Hutchings Psychiatric Center
Hutchinson Area Vocational
    Technical Institute

IBM Corporation
I.D.S./Investors Diversified
    Services
INA Corporation
IPCO Dental Division
IRS National Training Center
ITEL
ITS Video
ITT Continental Baking Inc.
Illinois Bell Telephone
Illinois College of Podiatric
    Medicine
Illinois Farm Bureau
Illinois Masonic Medical Center
Illinois State Police Training
    Academy
Illinois State University
Indiana Area School District

Indiana Bell Telephone
Indiana State University
Indiana University/Bloomington
Indiana University
    School of Dentistry
Indiana University
    School of Medicine
Indiana University School of
    Nursing
Indiana University/South Bend
Industrial Training Corporation
Inland Motor Divisions
Inland Steel Company
Institute for Education & Training
Insurance Service Office
Intel Corporation
International Communication
    Agency
International Harvester
    Photographic Center
International Paper Company
International Salt Company
Iowa Lakes Community College
Iowa Public Service Company
Iowa State University
Ithaca College (WICB-TV)

J&L Steel Corp.
JRB Associates
Jackson County Education
    Service District
Jackson State Community College
James Madison University
    Television
Jefferson Community College
Jefferson County Public Schools
Jersey Central Power & Light Co.
Jersey City State College-Centec
Jet Propulsion Laboratory/FEC
Johns Hopkins Medical School
Johns-Manville Corporation
Johnson & Johnson
S.C. Johnson & Son, Inc.
Johnson Controls, Inc.
Johnson County Community
    College

Johnston High School
Joliet Township High Schools

KFC Corporation
KLVW
Kaiser Aluminum & Chemical
Corp.
Kaiser Steel Corporation
Kamehameha School
Kansas State University
Kearney & Truker
J.P. Keefe Regional School
District
Kellogg Community College
Kellogg Company
Kelly-Springfield Tire Co.
Kemper Insurance Companies
Kennesaw College
Kent State University
Charles F. Kettering Foundation
Kettering Medical Center
Kingsboro Psychiatric Center
Video Productions
Kirkwood Community College
Kirtland Community College
Library
Klaus Radio & Electric Company
Kulicke & Sofia Industries
Kutztown State College (KSC-TV)

The Lacy Institute
Lake Forest High School
Lakeland Community College
Lakeshore Technical Institute
Lakewood City Schools
Lane Community College
LaSalle College
Laventhal & Horwath
Lawrence Livermore Laboratory
Lazarus
Learning Resource Center
Lebow Labs Audio Video, Inc.
Lehn & Fink Products Company
Le Moyne College
Lenox Hill Hospital
Lenox Industries, Inc.

Levi Straus & Co.
Lewis-Clark State College
The Liberty Corporation
Liberty Mutual Insurance
Company
Liberty Studio
Lincoln National Life
Insurance Co.
Lincoln National Television
Lindberg Productions, Inc.
Linn Benton Community College
J. Lipsey & Associates
Thomas J. Lipton, Inc.
Liqui-Box Corp.
Little Company of Mary Hospital
Lloyds Bank California
Lockheed Aircraft Service
Company
Loma Linda University
Long Beach Museum of Art
Long Island University-Brooklyn
Lord & Taylor
Los Angeles County
Los Angeles Pierce College
Los Angeles Police Department
Los Angeles Valley College
Louisiana Educational TV
Authority
Louisiana State University
Louisiana State University
Medical Center
Loyola University
Lutheran Church in America
Lyons Township High School
Lyons Township High School
South
MCQ Teleproduction
3M
3M/Business Products, Television
Dept.
Macsteel
Macy's New York
James Madison University
Madonna College
Maine Medical Center
Mamaroneck High School

Manufacturers Hanover Trust
Company
Manufacturers Life Insurance
Company
Maple Heights High School-
Media
Maplewood Junior High
Maritime Institute of Technology
and Graduate Studies
Marketdyne, International
Marriott Corp.
Marquette University
Marshalls
Marshall Field & Company
Martin Luther King Jr. General
Hospital L.A. County
Maryland Center for Public
Broadcasting
Maryland State Department of
Education
Marywood College
Massachusetts Board of Library
Commissioners
Massachusetts Educational TV
Massachusetts General Hospital
Massachusetts Mutual Life
Insurance Company
Massachusetts Rehabilitation
Commission
Master Builders Div./Martin
Marietta
May Company
The Maytag Company
Mayo Clinic
McDonald's Systems, Inc.
Mead Paper Group of Mead
Corporation
Medi-Share
Medical Audio Visual Services
Medical Care Development, Inc.
Medical College of Georgia
Medical University of South
Carolina
Meier & Frank Co.
Memorial Hospital System
Memorial University

Memphis State University
Mercer County Community
College
Mercer University
Merchants Insurance Group Inc.
Merck Sharp & Dohme
International
Mercy College of Detroit
Mercy College (IA)
Mercy Hospital (PA)
Mercy Hospital and Medical
Center (IL)
Merrill Lynch
Mervyn's
Methacton School District
Methodist Hospital (NY)
Methodist Hospital (TX)
Metro High School
Metro Instructional TV
Metropolitan Life Insurance
Metropolitan State College
Metropolitan Technical
Community College
Miami-Dade Community College-
North Campus
Miami University
Michigan Bell
Michigan Department of
Education
Michigan State University
College of Osteopathic
Medicine
Michigan State University
Television (WKAR-TV/ITV)
Middle County Central School
District #11
Midland Public Schools
Military Airlift Command USAF
Millipore Corporation
Milwaukee Area Technical
College
City of Milwaukee Health
Department
Milwaukee Regional Medical
Instructional Television
Station, Inc.

Mine Safety Appliances Company
Minnesota Cable
Communications Board
Minnesota Department of Transportation
Minnesota Zoological Garden
Mississippi School Supply
Mississippi State University
Mississippi University for Women
Missouri Department of
Education-State Schools for
Severely Handicapped
Missouri Southern State College
Mobil
Mobil Video-One
Model Secondary School of
the Deaf
Mohawk Valley Community
College
Molex, Inc.
Molner & Company Advertising
Inc.
Mona Shores Schools
Monsanto Company
Montana State University
Montclair State College
Montgomery County Community
College
Montgomery Ward
Monumental Films & Recordings
Inc.
Moorpark College
Moraine Valley Community
College
Moravian College
Morehead State University
Robert Morris College
Mother Macauley High
School
Motorola Communications and
Electronics
Mountain Bell Training Center
Mount Carmel Medical Center
Mount Vernon College
Mundelein College
Muskegon Community College

Mutual Life Insurance Company
of New York
Mutual of Omaha

NAS
NASA
NH&S
NIPSCO
NML Insurance Co.
NUS Corporation
Nabisco Inc
Nassau Community College
Nassau County Police Department
National Gallery of Art
National Institute for
Occupational Safety & Health
National Medical Audio Visual
Center
National Science Foundation
Nationwide Insurance Company
Naval Air Development Center
Nazareth College of Rochester
Nebraska Veterans Administration TV Network
Neiman Marcus
New Covenant Fellowship
New England Baptist Hospital
New England Institute of
Technology
New England Mutual Life
Insurance Company
New England Telephone
New England Telephone Learning
Center
New Hampshire Public Television
New Jersey Division of Criminal
Justice
New Jersey Dept. of Health
New Jersey Institute of
Technology
New Jersey Medical School
New Mexico State University
New Trier Television
New York City Police Department

New York Life Insurance
Company
New York Medical College
New York Network
New York State Department of
Correctional Services
(CSET-TV)
New York State Education
Department
New York State Psychiatric
Institute
New York University School of
the Arts
Newark Beth Israel Medical
Center
Newark High School (WNHS-TV)
Newman Visual Education Inc.
Newport-Mesa Unified School
District
Niagara County Community
College
Niagara Mohawk Power
Corporation
Niagara University
Norden Systems
North Adams State College
North Carolina A&T State
University
North Carolina State
University
North Central Texas Regional
Police Academy
North Dakota State University
North West Federal Savings &
Loan
Northhampton County Area
Community College
Northeast Illinois University
Northeast Missouri State
University
Northeast Utilities
Northern Illinois University
Northern Kentucky University
Northern Natural Gas
Northern New Mexico
Community College

Northland Pioneer College
Northrop Corporation Aircraft
Group
Northrop Corportion Electro-
Mechanical Division
Northwest Missouri State
University
Northwest Natural Gas Co.
Northwestern Bell
Northwestern Memorial Hospital
Northwestern Mutual Life
Norton Company
Nova University

OTB Capital District Regional
Off Track Betting Corporation
Oakland Community College
Oakton Community College
O'Berry Center
Odessa College
Ohio Bell Telephone Company
The Ohio State University College
of Medicine
Ohio University-College of
Osteopathic Medicine
Ohio University
Ohio Valley Medical Microwave
Television System
Oklahoma Gas and Electric
Company
Oklahoma Natural Gas Co.
Old Dominion University
Olin Corporation
Olivet Nazarene College
Omega School of
Communications
Orange Coast College
Oregon Institute of Technology
Orlando Regional Medical Center
Ortho Diagnostics, Inc.
Oshkosh Area School District
Osseo TV/Productions
Outlet Department Stores
Owens-Corning Fiberglas
Corporation
Owens-Illinois, Inc.

PBS
PPG Industries, Inc.
Pacific Fleet Audio Visual
   Command
Pacific Gas and Electric Company
Pacific Lutheran University
Pacific Mutual
Pacific Northwest Bell
Pacific Power & Light
Pacific Telephone Company
Pacific University
Paine Webber
Palmyra Area School District
L.D. Pankey Institute
Paramus Public Schools
   E.D.C.
Park College
Parma Instructional Television
Pastoral Communications
Pee Dee Area Health Education
   Center
Penn Mutual Life Insurance
   Company
J.C. Penney Company (GA)
J.C. Penney Company (NY)
Pennsylvania College of Podiatric
   Medicine
Pennsylvania Power and Light
   Co.
Pennsylvania State University
Pennzoil Company
The Peoples Gas Light and Coke
   Co.
Pepsico
Pfizer, Inc.
Philadelphia College of
   Osteopathic Medicine
Philadelphia College of Textiles &
   Science
Philadelphia School District
Philip Morris Training Center
   (KY)
Philip Morris Training Center
   (VA)
Philips Medical Systems, Inc.
Philips Petroleum Company

Phoenix Mutual Life Insurance
   Company
James Picker Center for
   Continuing Education
Piper Aircraft Corp.
Pittsfield School Department
Pius XI High School
Plymouth Public Library
Ponderosa System Inc.
Pontiac Motor Division
Portland General Electric Co.
Portland State University
Practising Law Institute
Prairie State College
H.C. Prange Co.
Pratt & Whitney Aircraft Group
Pratt & Whitney Aircraft
   Commercial Products Div.
Pratt & Whitney Aircraft
   Manufacturing Div.
Pratt & Whitney Aircraft Service
   School
Price Waterhouse & Company
Prince George's Community
   College
Project Occupations
Providence Hospital School of
   Nursing
The Prudential Insurance
   Company
Public Safety Dept.Region XIV
Public Service Company of New
   Mexico
Puerto Rico-Social Services
Pullman Kellogg
Punxsutawney Area Schools
Purdue University

The Quaker Oats Company

RB Furniture
RCA Corporation
R.L.D.S. World Church
   Headquarters
Radford College
Ralston-Purina

Ralston-Purina-Food Maker
Division
Ralston-Purina Grocery
Products Division
Ramada Inn, Inc.
Rancho Amigos Hospital
Ravenswood Hospital
Raytheon Data Systems
Recognition Equipment Inc.
Reden Laboratories Inc.
Redwood High School
Reliance Electric Company
Reserve Mining Co.
Rexnord Co.
J. Sargeant Reynolds Community
College
Reynolds Metals Company
R.J. Reynolds Tobacco
Rhode Island Department of
State Library Services
Rhode Island Junior College
Rich's
Richardson Independent School
District TV Center
Richmond Public Schools
Richway Stores
Rike's
Rio Hondo College
Riverside Brookfield High School
Roadway Express, Inc.
Rochester Institute of Technology
Rochester Methodist Hospital
Rockland Research Institute
Rockwell International
Rohm and Hass Company
Roosevelt University
Ross-Gaffney Inc.
Royal Bank of Canada
Rush-Presbyterian
Rutgers-The State University of
New Jersey

SCM Corporation
S/T Videocassette Duplicating
Sacred Heart Medical Center
Safeco Insurance Company

St. Andrews Presbyterian College
St. Cloud State University
St Francis Hospital (IL)
St. Francis Hospital (WI)
St. Gabriel's Hall
St. John Brebeuf
St. John's Hospital (MN)
St. John's Hospital (IL)
St. John's Mercy Medical Center
St. John's Regional Health Center
St. Joseph College (CT)
St. Joseph's College (IN)
St. Joseph's Hospital (FL)
St. Joseph Hospital (IL)
St. Joseph Hospital (TX)
St. Joseph Mercy Hospital
St. Louis Community College at
Florissant Valley
St. Luke's Methodist Hospital
St. Petersburg Junior College
St. Regis Paper Company
Saks Fifth Avenue
Salem School District Media
Services
Sambo's Restaurant
San Antonio College
San Bernardino County
San Diego Community College
San Diego State University
San Diego Unified School District
San Francisco State University
San Jose State University
Sanders Associates
Sandia Laboratories
Sangamon State University
Sanger Harris Department Stores
Sargent College of Allied Health
Professions
Satchidananda Ashiam-Yogaville
Inc.
Sauk Valley College
Save the Children
Scarlet Oaks C.D.C.
Schlumberger Well Services
School of Basic Medical Science
Searle Radio Graphics

Sears Roebuck & Company
Seattle City Light
Seattle Public Library
Sedco Inc.
Seton Hall University
Shapiro Development Center
    (KDC TV3)
Shelby State Community College
Sheldon Jackson College
Sheridan College
Shillto's Department Store
Sikorsky Aircraft
Sioux Falls School District 49-5
Sisters of Charity Hospital
Slow Scan TV
A.O. Smith Corporation
Smithkline Corporation
Smithsonian Institution
Joe Snyder & Co., Ltd.
Solano Community College
Solar Turbines International
Sony Corporation of America
Sorgel-Lee-Riordan
Source Services Corporation
South Beach Psychiatric Center
South Carolina Educational
    Resources
South Carolina Educational
    Television Network
South Eastern Michigan
    Telecommunications
South Hadley Library System
South Hills Health System
Southeast Community
    College
Southern Bell Telephone
Southern California Gas
    Company
Southern Connecticut State
    College
Southern Illinois University
    School of Medicine
Southern Methodist University
Southern Missionary College
Southern New England
    Telephone

Southern Pacific Transportation
    Company
Southern Railway
Southern West Virginia
    Community College
Southfield-Lathrop High School
Southwest Boston Community
    Services, Inc.
Southwest Missouri State
    University
Southwestern Bell
Southwestern Life Insurance
    Company
Southerwestern Public Service
    Company
ISS-Sperry/Univac
Sperry/Univac (MN)
Sperry/Univac (NJ)
E.R. Squibb & Sons, Inc.
The Standard Oil Company
Standard Oil Company of Indiana
Stanford University
Stark Technical College
State Accident Insurance Fund
State Compensation Insurance
    Fund
State Fair Community College
State Farm Insurance Company
State Mutual Life Assurance
    Company of America
State Technical Institute at
    Memphis
State University of New York
    at Albany
State University of New York
    at Alfred
State University of New York
    at Binghamton
State University of New York
    at Buffalo
State University of New York,
    College of Arts & Sciences
State University of New York
    Dutchess Community College
State University of New York at
    New Paltz

State University of New York
   at Oneonta
State University of New York
   at Plattsburgh
State University of New York
   at Potsdam
State University of New York
   at Purchase
State University of New York
   at Stony Brook
State University of New York
   Upstate Medical Center
Stauffer Chemical Company
Stephens College
Stephenson School Supply
   Company
Sterling Drugs
J.P. Stevens & Company Inc.
Stockton State College
Strake Jesuit
Strawbridge & Clothier
Suffolk County Police Academy
Sun Land Center
Sun Life Assurance Company
   of Canada
Sweda International
Swiss Colony Stores, Inc.
Syncrude Canada, Ltd.
Syntex Laboratories, Inc.
Syracuse University

TPF&C
TRW Industrial & Replacement
TAGER
Tarrant County Jr. College
Taylor Instrument Company
Tektronix Inc.
Teleprompter Manhattan
   Productions
Teletype Corporation
Temple University
Temple University Medical School
Temple University School of
   Pharmacy
Tenafly Board of Education
Texaco, Inc.

Texas Christian University
Texas Christian University
   (KTCU-FM)
Texas Credit Union & Affiliates
Texas Department of Public
   Safety
Texas Eastern Corporation
Texas Eastern School of Nursing
Texas Heart Institute Television
   Facility
Texas Instruments, Inc.
Texas Research Institute of
   Mental Sciences
Texas Southmost College
Texas State Bar
Texas State Library
Texas Tech University School of
   Medicine
Texas Utilities Services, Inc.
Texas Wesleyan College
Thalhimer Brothers, Inc.
Thalner Electronic Laboratories,
   Inc.
Thatcher Glass Manufacturing
   Co.
Thornton Community School
Tidewater Community College
Timex Corporation
The Timken Company
Timken Mercy Medical Center
The Trane Company
The Travellers Insurance
   Company
Tri-State Oil Tool Industry, Inc.
Trident Technical College
Truckstops of America
Tucson Medical Center
Tuft's Educational Media Center

Union Carbide Corporation (NY)
Union Carbide Corporation (OH)
Union Carbide Corporation (WV)
Union Carbide Corporation
   Linde Division
Union Carbide Corporation
   Metals Division

Union Carbide Nuclear Division
Union Electric Company
Union Pacific Railroad
Union Trust Company
United Energy Resources, Inc.
United Methodist
  Communications
United Presbyterian Church
U.S. Air Force Reserve
U.S. Army Engineering Division-
  South Atlantic
U.S. Army Signal Center at Fort
  Gordon
U.S. Coast Guard Academy
U.S. Department of Agriculture
U.S. General Accounting Office
U.S. Department of Interior
U.S. Department of Labor
U.S. Food and Drug Adminis-
  tration/Bureau Medical Devices
U.S. Food and Drug
  Administration
U.S. Gypsum Company
U.S. Military Academy
U.S. Naval Academy
U.S. Navy Internal Related
  Activity
U.S. Navy Multimedia
U.S. Office of Education, HEW
U.S. Public Health Service
  Hospital
U.S. Trust Company of New York
United Telecom Service, Inc.
United Way Productions
Unity Hospital
University of Alabama
University of Alabama Television
  Services
University of Alaska at Anchorage
University of Alaska at Fairbanks
University of Arizona
University of Arizona
  Microcampus
University of Arkansas
University of Bridgeport
University of California-

Educational TV
University of California at
  Berkeley
University of California at Davis
University of California at
  Los Angeles
University of California at
  San Diego
University of Central Florida
University of Chicago
University of Colorado Medical
  Center
University of Colorado Television
University of Connecticut
University of D.C.
University of Delaware
University of Denver
University of Florida
University of Georgia
University of Houston
University of Idaho
University of Illinois
University of Illinois at
  Urbana-Champaign
University of Iowa
University of Iowa-University
  Video Center
University of Kansas
University of Kansas School of
  Medicine at Wichita
University of Kentucky
University of Louisville
University of Maine-Augusta
University of Maryland
University of Massachusetts-
  Center for Media Development
University of Massachusetts
University of Miami
University of Michigan
University of Minnesota
University of Minnesota-
  Technical College
University of Missouri
University of Missouri-Kansas
  City School of Medicine
University of Nebraska at Lincoln

University of Nebraska Television
(KUON-TV)
University of Nevada at Reno
University of North Carolina at
Chapel Hill
University of North Carolina at
Greensboro
University of North Dakota
University of Northern Iowa
University of Oklahoma
University of Pennsylvania
University of Pittsburgh
University of Pittsburgh at
Johnstown
University of Puget Sound
University of Richmond
University of the Sacred Heart
University of South Carolina
University of South Dakota
University of Southern California
University of Southern Florida
University of Southern Mississippi
University of Tennessee
University of Texas at Austin
University of Texas Closed-Circuit
Television
University of Texas, Health
Science Center/Dallas
University of Texas (El Paso)
University of Texas (Houston)
University of Texas (San Antonio)
The University of Toledo
The University of Tulsa
University of Utah Instructional
Media Services
University of Vermont Instruc-
tional Development Center-
Video Unit
University of Vermont Extension
Service
University of Virginia
University of Washington
University of Wisconsin
(Eau Clair)
University of Wisconsin
(Green Bay)

University of Wisconsin
(Madison)
University of Wisconsin
(Menasha)
University of Wisconsin
(Milwaukee)
University of Wisconsin
(Oshkosh)
University of Wisconsin
(Platteville)
University of Wisconsin
(River Falls)
University of Wisconsin at Stout
Univision
Urban Academy
Utah State University Radio and
Television

Valdosta State College
Van Camp Seafood
Vanity Fair Mills, Inc.
Veterans Administration Hospital
(CA)
Veterans Administration Hospital
(CT)
Veterans Administration Hospital
(MO)
Veterans Administration (ND)
Veterans Administration Medical
Center (AL)
Veterans Administration Medical
Center (CA)
Veterans Administration-Brent-
wood Medical Center (CA)
Veterans Administration Medical
Center (IL)
Veterans Administration Medical
Center (KY)
Veterans Administration Medical
& Regional Office Center (ME)
Veterans Administration Medical
Center (MD)
Veterans Administration Hospital
(MA)
Veterans Administration Medical
Center (MN)

Veterans Administration Hospital (NE)

Veterans Administration Medical Center (NY)

Veterans Administration Medical Center (NY)

Veterans Administration Medical Center (TX)

Veterans Administration Medical Center (TX)

Veterans Administration Medical Center (UT)

Veterans Administration Medical Center (WI)

Veterans Center, Olin & Teague Branch (TX)

Villanova University

Virginia Beach City Public Schools

Virginia Commonwealth University

Virginia Electric & Power Company

Virginia Mason Hospital

Virginia State University

Virginia Technical Learning Resources Center

WENH-TV

WNJU-TV

Walgreen Company

Walter Reed Army Medical Center

Wappingers Central Media

Wards Company

Warren, Muller, Dolobowsky, Inc.

Washburn University

Washington County Board of Education

Washington Gas Light

Washington Mutual Savings Bank

Washington State Government

Washington State Department of Social & Health Services

Washington State University

Washington University Medical School

Waubonsee Community College

Wayne County Intermediate School District

Wayne Township Schools Television Center

Weber State College

Weirton Steel

Wendy's International

Wellfleet Public Library

Wescom Inc.

Wesley Medical Center

School District of West Allis-West Milwaukee

West Chemical Products, Inc.

West Chicago High School

West Hartford Public Schools

West Point-Pepperell, Inc.

West Virginia Library Commission Video Services

West Virginia University Medical Center Television

Western Connecticut State College

Western Electric Company

Western Geophysical

Western Illinois University

Western Kentucky University

Western Michigan University

Western Psychiatric Institute & Clinic

Western Wisconsin Technical Institute

Westinghouse Defense & Electronic Systems Center

Westinghouse Electric Corporation

Westinghouse Marine Division

Westside Community Schools

Weyerhauser Company

Wheat First Securities

Wheaton College

Wheaton Warrenville High School

Whirlpool Corporation

Wichita State University

Wickes Furniture

J.S. Wiener & Associates

Willis Engineering
Window Rock School District #8
Windsor Board of Education
Winkelman Stores, Inc.
Winn-Dixie Food Stores, Inc.
Winston-Salem, City of
Wisconsin Electric Power
    Company
Wisconsin Natural Resources
    Department
Daniel Woodhead, Inc.
Woodward Academy Television
Woodward & Lothrop
Worcester Controls Corporation
Worcester Polytechnic Institute
Worcester State College
World Book/ Childcraft Inter-
    national Inc.
World University
Wright State University
Wurlitzer Company
Wyoming Department of
    Education
Wyoming Family Practice
    Program

X-Pert Enterprise
Xavier University Television
Xerox Corportion

Yonkers Board of Education
Youngstown Sheet & Tube
    Company

Appendix C
Manufacturers of Video Equipment

The following manufacturers are listed in the 1979-80 edition of *The Video Register*. (The 1980-81 edition, with additional listings and more complete information, will be available from Knowledge Industry Publications in the fall of 1980.)

ADDA CORP.
1671 Dell Ave.
Campbell, CA 95008

THE ADVANCE PRODUCTS CO.
PO Box 2178
1101 E. Central
Wichita, KS 67201

ADVENT CORP.
195 Albany St.
Cambridge, MA 02139

AKAI AMERICA LTD.
(Div. of Akai Electric, Japan)
2139 E. Del Amo Blvd.
Compton, CA 90224

ALLEN AVIONICS, INC.
(Div. of A.K. Allen Co.)
224 E. Second St.
Mineola, NY 11501

AMARAY SALES CORP.
1901 Old Middlefield Way,
Suite 11
Mountain View, CA 94043

AMCO ENGINEERING CO.
3801 N. Rose St.
Schiller Park, IL 60176

AMERICAN DATA CORP.
(Div. of North America Philips
Corp., New York, NY)
401 Wynn Dr.
Huntsville, AL 35805

AMERICAN SATELLITE CORP.
(Subs. of Fairchild Industries)
20301 Century Blvd.
Germantown, MD 20767

AMPEREX ELECTRONIC CORP.
(Div. of North American Philips
Corp., New York, NY)
PO Box 278
Slatersville, RI 02876

AMPEX CORP.
401 Broadway
Redwood City, CA 94063

AMTRON CORP.
PO Box 1150
Freedom Blvd.
Aptos, CA 95003

ANDREW CORP.
10500 W. 153 St.
Orland Park, IL 60462

ANGENIEUX CORP. OF AMERICA
1500 Ocean Ave.
Bohemia, NY 11716

ANTON/BAUER INC.
66 Center St.
Shelton, CT 06484

ANVIL CASES, INC.
4128 Temple City Blvd.
Rosemead, CA 91770

ARVIN/ECHO SCIENCE CORP.
(Div. of Arvin Industries
Columbus, IN)
485 E. Middlefield Rd.
Mountain View, CA 94043

ASACA CORP. OF AMERICA
(Div. of Asaca Corp., Shibasoku
Co., Ltd., Japan)
1289 Rand Rd.
Des Plaines, IL 60016

AUDIOTRONICS VIDEO DISPLAY DIVISION
(Div. of Audiotronics Corp.,
North Hollywood, CA)
530 Fifth Ave., NW
New Brighton, MN 55112

AVL DIGITAL LTD.
70 Milner Ave., #5
Scarborough, Ontario MIS 3P8

BALL ELECTRONIC DISPLAY DIVISION
PO Box 43376
St. Paul, MN 55164

BARDWELL McALISTER, INC.
(Div. of F.B. Ceco)
7269 Santa Monica Blvd.
Hollywood, CA 90046

BASF SYSTEMS
(Div. of BASF Wyandotte Corp.)
Crosby Dr.
Bedford, MA 01730

BASF VIDEO CORP.
(Div. of BASF Wyandotte Corp.)
1800 Quail St.
Newport Beach, CA 92660

BERKEY COLORTRAN, INC.
(Div. of Berkey Photo, Inc.)
1015 Chestnut St.
Burbank, CA 91502

BESTON ELECTRONICS INC.
PO Box 106A
15315 S. Highway 169
Olathe, KS 66061

BETA SIGMA CORP./ VIDCOM
2711 E. Indian School Rd.
Phoenix, AZ 85016

BJA SYSTEMS, INC.
666 Davisville Rd.
Willow Grove, PA 19090

BLACKBOURN INC.
10150 Crosstown Circle
Eden Prairie, MN 55344

BRETFORD MANUFAC-TURING, INC.
9715 Soreng Ave.
Schiller Park, IL 60176

BROADCAST VIDEO SYSTEMS LTD.
1050 McNichol Ave.
Agincourt, Ontario M1W 2L8

BSC INC.
2932 River Rd.
River Grove, IL 60171

BTX CORP.
438 Boston Post Rd.
Weston, MA 02193

BUHL OPTICAL
1009 Beech Ave.
Pittsburgh, PA 15233

CANON U.S.A., INC., OPTICS DIVISION
(Division of Canon, Inc., Japan)
10 Nevada Dr.
Lake Success, NY 11040

CAPRON LIGHTING AND SOUND
278 West St.
Needham, MA 02194

C-COR ELECTRONICS, INC.
60 Decibel Rd.
State College, PA 16801

CENTRAL DYNAMICS CORP.
(Div. of Central Dynamics Ltd.,
Montreal, Canada)
331 W. Northwest Highway
Palatine, IL 60067

CEZAR INTERNATIONAL, LTD.
491 Marcara Ave.
Suite 1003
Sunnyvale, CA 94086

CHRISTIE ELECTRIC CORP.
3410 W. 67 St.
Los Angeles, CA 90043

CHYRON CORP.
265 Bethpage/Spagnoli Rd.
Melville, NY 11747

CINE 60 INC.
630 Ninth Ave.
New York, NY 10036

CINEMA PRODUCTS CORP.
2037 Granville Ave.
Los Angeles, CA 90025

CLEAR-COM INTERCOM SYSTEMS
759 Harrison St.
San Francisco, CA 94107

CMX SYSTEMS
(Div. of Orrox Corp.)
3303 Scott Blvd.
Santa Clara, CA 95050

COHU, INC., ELECTRONICS DIVISION
5725 Kearny Villa Rd.
San Diego, CA 92123

COLORADO VIDEO, INC.
PO Box 928
Boulder, CO 80306

COMMAND PRODUCTS CO.
PO Box 1577
Evanston, IL 60204

COMMERCIAL ELEC-TRONICS, INC.
880 Maude Ave.
Mountain View, CA 94043

COMPREHENSIVE VIDEO SUPPLY
148 Veterans Dr.
Northvale, NJ 07647

CONCORD COMMUNICA-TIONS SYSTEMS
790 Park Ave.
Huntington, NY 11743

CONRAC, BENJAMIN ELEC-TRONICS
49 Smith St.
Farmingdale, NJ 11735

CONRAC CORPORATION CONRAC DIVISION
600 N. Rimsdale Ave.
Covina, CA 91722

**CONRAC CORP. SYSTEMS-
EAST DIVISION**
32 Fairchild Ave.
West Caldwell, NJ 07006

**CONSOLIDATED VIDEO
SYSTEMS INC.**
1255 E. Arques Ave.
Sunnyvale, CA 94086

CONVERGENCE CORP.
1641 McGaw
Irvine, CA 92714

CROSS POINT LATCH
316 Broad St.
Summit, NJ 07901

DATATRON, INC.
1562 Reynolds Ave.
Irvine, CA 92714

**DIELECTRIC COMMUNI-
CATIONS**
(Unit of General Signal)
Tower Hill Rd.
Raymond, ME 04071

DIGITAL VIDEO SYSTEMS
716 Gordon Baker Rd.
Willowdale, Ontario, Canada
M2H 3B4

DYNAIR ELECTRONICS, INC.
5275 Market St.
San Diego, CA 92114

DYNASCIENCES
(Div. of Whittaker Corp., Los
Angeles, CA)
Township Line Rd.
Blue Bell, PA 19422

DYTEK INDUSTRIES, INC.
2492 W. Second Ave.
Denver, CO 80223

ECHOLAB, INC.
175 Bedford Rd.
Burlington, MA 01803

EDUTRON INC.
25 Oak St. Suite 1
Roswell, GA 30075

**E.I. DU PONT DE NEMOURS
& CO., INC.**
(Magnetic Products Div.)
Du Pont Airport Site
Building #1
Wilmington, DE 19898

EIGEN VIDEO
PO Box 1027
Grass Valley, CA 95945

ELECTRO CONTROLS, INC.
2975 S. 300 West
Salt Lake City, UT 84115

ELECTROHOME LTD.
809 Wellington St. N.
Kitchener, Ontario, Canada
N2G 4J6

**ELECTRO & OPTICAL
SYSTEMS LTD.**
3015 Kennedy Rd., Unit #12
Scarborough, Ontario M1V 1E7

ESE
142 Sierra St.
El Segunda, CA 90245

FERNSEH GROUP
(Div. of Robert Bosch Corp.)
279 Midland Ave.
Saddle Brook, NJ 07662

**FIBERBILT PHOTO
PRODUCTS**
(Div. of Ikelheimer Ernst, Inc.)
601 W. 26 St.
New York, NY 10001

FIDELIPAK
109 Gaither Dr.
Mt. Laurel, NJ 08057

**FREZZOLINI ELECTRONICS,
INC.**
7 Valley St.
Hawthorne, NJ 07506

**FRYAN AUDIO VISUAL
EQUIPMENT INC.**
4369 Hamann Parkway
Willoughby, OH 44094

**FUJI MAGNETIC TAPE
DIVISION**
(Div. of Fuji Photo Film USA,
Inc.)
350 Fifth Ave.
New York, NY 10016

FUJINON OPTICAL, INC.
(Div. of Fuji Photo Optical Co.,
Ltd., Japan)
672 White Plains Rd.
Scarsdale, NY 10583

GARNER INDUSTRIES
4200 N. 48 St.
Lincoln, NE 68504

GBC CCTV CORP.
315 Hudson St.
New York, NY 10013

**GENERAL ELECTRIC CO.
VIDEO DISPLAY EQUIP-
MENT OPERATION**
Electronics Park 6-206
Syracuse, NY 13221

**GENERAL ELECTRIC
LIGHTING BUSINESS GROUP**
Nela Park
Cleveland, OH 44112

GOTHAM AUDIO CORP.
741 Washington Ave.
New York, NY 10014

**THE GRASS VALLEY GROUP
INC.**
(Div. of Tektronix, Inc.,
Beaverton, OR)
PO Box 1114
Bitney Springs Rd.
Grass Valley, CA 95945

**THE GREAT AMERICAN
MARKET**
PO Box 178
21133 Costanso St.
Woodland Hills, CA 91364

GRUBER PRODUCTS CO.
5254 Jackman Rd.
Toledo, OH 43613

**HARRIS CORP. BROADCAST
PRODUCTS DIVISION**
(Div. of Harris Corp., Melbourne,
FL)
PO Box 4290
Quincy, IL 62301

**HITACHI DENSHI AMERICA,
LTD.**
175 Crossways Park W.
Woodbury, NY 11797

H. WILSON CO.
555 W. Taft Dr.
South Holland, IL 60473

IDS
PO Box 581
Willow & Valley Rds.
Boyertown, PA 19512

**IKEGAMI ELECTRONICS
(USA), INC.**
(Div. of Ikegami Tsushinki Co.,
Tokyo, Japan)
37 Brook Ave.
Maywood, NJ 07607

IKELHEIMER-ERNST, INC.
601 W. 26 St.
New York, NY 10001

IMAGE DEVICES INC.
1825 NE 149 St.
Miami, FL 33181

IMAGE MAGNIFICATION, INC.
739 Airway Circle
New Smyrna Beach, FL 31069

IMPACT COMMUNCATIONS, INC.
9202 Markville Dr.
Dallas, TX 75243

INDUSTRIAL SCIENCES, INC.
PO Box 1495
Gainesville, FL 32602

INTERAND CORP.
(Div. of Instructional Dynamics, Inc.)
666 N. Lake Shore Dr.
Chicago, IL 60611

INTERNATIONAL MICRO-WAVE CORP.
33 River Rd.
Cos Cob, CT 06807

INTERNATIONAL NUCLEAR CORP.
608 Norris Ave.
Nashville, TN 37204

INTERNATIONAL VIDEO CORP.
455 W. Maude Ave.
Sunnyvale, CA 94086

ITI ELECTRONICS, INC.
PO Box 260
369 Lexington Ave.
Clifton, NJ 07011

JATEX, INC.
9202 B Markville
Dallas, TX 75243

JVC CORP.
See U.S. JVC Corporation

KALART VICTOR CORP.
Hultenius St.
Plainville, CT 06062

K AND H PRODUCTS, LTD.
PO Box 246
North Bennington, VT 05257

KAPCO ENTERPRISES
947 Janesville Ave.
Ft. Atkinson, WI 53538

KINGS ELECTRONICS CO., INC.
40 Marbledale Rd.
Tuckahoe, NY 10707

KLIEGL BROTHERS
32-32 48 Ave.
Long Island City, NY 11101

KNOX VIDEO PRODUCTS
9700B George Palmer Highway
Lanham, MD 20801

LAIRD TELEMEDIA, INC.
2125 S.W. Temple
Salt Lake City, UT 84115

LEE-RAY INDUSTRIES, INC.
38 E. First St.
Mesa, AZ 85202

LEITCH VIDEO LTD.
705 Progress Ave., Unit 46
Scarborough, Ontario, Canada
M1H 2X1

LISTEC TELEVISION EQUIP-
MENT
39 Cain Dr.
Plainview, NY 11803

LOWEL-LIGHT MANU-
FACTURING INC.
421 W. 54 St.
New York, NY 10019

LUXOR CORP.
2245 Delany Rd.
Waukegan, IL 60085

L-W INTERNATIONAL
6416 Variel Ave.
Woodland Hills, CA 91367

3M/MAGNETIC AUDIO-
VIDEO PRODUCTS
(Div. of 3M Co.)
3M Center
St. Paul, MN 55101

3M/MINCOM VIDEO
PRODUCTS
3M Center
St. Paul, MN 55101

MAGNAVOX CONSUMER
ELECTRONICS CO.
(Div. of North American
Philips Corp., New York, NY)
1700 Magnavox Way
Fort Wayne, IN 46804

MARCONI ELECTRONICS,
INC.
100 Stonehurst Court
Northvale, NJ 07647

MARSHALL ELECTRONICS
PO Box 2027
Culver City, CA 90230

MAST DEVELOPMENT CO.
2212 E. 12 St.
Davenport, IA 52803

MAXELL CORP. OF
AMERICA
60 Oxford Dr.
Moonachie, NJ 07074

MEDIA CONCEPTS, INC.
559 49 St. S.
St. Petersburg, FL 33707

MEMOREX CORP.
PO Box 1000
1200 Memorex Dr.
Santa Clara, CA 95052

MERLIN ENGINEERING
WORKS, INC.
1880 Embarcadero Rd.
Palo Alto, CA 94303

MICRO CONSULTANTS, INC.
2483 E. Bayshore Rd., #209
Palo Alto, CA 94303

MICROTIME INC.
(Subs. of Anderson Group, Inc.)
1280 Blue Hills Ave.
Bloomfield, CT 06002

MICROTRAN CO., INC.
145 E. Mineola Ave.
PO Box 236
Valley Stream, NY 11582

MICROWAVE ASSOCIATES
63 Third Ave., Bldg. 5
Burlington, MA 01803

MID AMERICA PLASTICS
CORP.
6900 Canby, #108
Reseda, CA 91335

MILLER PROFESSIONAL
EQUIPMENT, INC.
10816 Burbank Blvd.
North Hollywood, CA 91601

MPB TECHNOLOGIES, INC.
PO Box 160
Ste. Anne de Bellevue
Quebec, Canada H9X 3L5

M.P. VIDEO
45 Kenneth St.
Newton, MA 02161

MSI TELEVISION
(Div. of COM TEL, Inc.
4788 S. State St.
Salt Lake City, UT 84107

NANOTEC
414 Hilmen Pl.
Solana Beach, CA 92075

NEC AMERICA, INC.
(Div. of Nippon Electric, Ltd.,
Tokyo, Japan)
Consumer Prod. Div.: Video
Products
130 Martin Lane
Elk Grove Village, IL 60007

**NEUMADE PRODUCTS
CORP.**
PO Box 568
720 White Plains Rd.
Scarsdale, NY 10583

**NORTH AMERICAN PHILIPS
CORP.**
100 E. 42 St.
New York, NY 10017

N.T.I. AMERICA, INC.
(Div. of Nippon Television
Industries, Japan)
1680 N. Vine St.
Hollywood, CA 90028

**O'CONNOR ENGINEERING
LABORATORIES**
100 Kalmus Dr.
Costa Mesa, CA 92626

OPTEK, INC.
1390 N. McCan St.
Anaheim, CA 92806

ORROX CORP.
3303 Scott Blvd.
Santa Clara, CA 95050

**PANASONIC CO., DIVISION
OF MATSUSHITA ELECTRIC
CORP. OF AMERICA**
Video Systems Division
1 Panasonic Way
Secaucus, NJ 07094

PANVIDICON, INC.
PO Box 71
Mansfield, MA 02048

PEERLESS SALES CO.
1950 Hawthorne Ave.
Melrose Park, IL 60160

**PHELPS DODGE CABLE &
WIRE CO.**
(Div. of Phelps Dodge, New York,
NY)
Foot of Point St.
Yonkers, NY 10702

**PHILIPS BROADCAST
EQUIPMENT CORP.**
(Div. of North American
Philips Corp., New York, NY)
91 McKee Dr.
Mahwah, NJ 07430

**PHILIPS TEST & MEASURING
INSTRUMENTS, INC.**
(Div. of North American
Philips Corp., New York, NY)
85 McKee Dr.
Mahwah, NJ 07430

PORTAC INC.
108 Aero Camino
Goleta, CA 93017

PORTA-PATTERN TELECOM-
MUNICATIONS INDUSTRIES
LTD.
6822 Santa Monica Blvd.
Los Angeles, CA 90038

POWER OPTICS
(Div. of Evershed Power Optics
Ltd., Surry, England)
1055 West Germantown Pike
Fairview Village, PA 19409

PROJECTION SYSTEMS, INC.
517 Van Houten Ave.
Passaic, NJ 07055

QUICK-SET INC.
3650 Woodhead Dr.
Northbrook, IL 60062

QSI SYSTEMS, INC.
993 Watertown St.
West Newton, MA 02165

Q-TV/TELESYNC
(Div. of Q-CO Industries Inc.)
33 W. 60 St.
New York, NY 10023

RAIL MANUFACTURING
CORP.
4559 Granite Dr.
Tucker, GA 30084

RANK PRECISION
INDUSTRIES INC.
411 E. Jarvis Ave.
Des Plaines, IL 60018

RCA CLOSED CIRCUIT VIDEO
EQUIPMENT
(Div. of RCA Corp., New York,
NY)
New Holland Ave.
Lancaster, PA 17604

RCA CORP. BROADCAST
SYSTEMS
Front & Cooper St., Bldg. 2-5
Camden, NJ 08102

RECORTEC, INC.
777 Palomar Ave.
Sunnyvale, CA 94086

RELIANCE PLASTICS &
PACKAGING
108-18 Queens Blvd.
Forest Hills, NY 11375

RESEARCH TECHNOLOGY,
INC.
4700 Chase Ave.
Lincolnwood, IL 60646

REYNOLDS/LETERON
13425 Wyandotte St.
North Hollywood, CA 91605

ROBOT RESEARCH, INC.
7591 Convoy Ct.
San Diego, CA 92111

ROHDE & SCHWARZ SALES
CO., INC.
14 Gloria La.
Fairfield, NJ 07006

ROSS VIDEO LTD.
PO Box 220
9 Plaza Dr.
Iroquois, Ontario, Canada
K0E 1K0

ROTARY COMPANY, INC.
1746 Dale Rd.
Buffalo, NY 14225

SANYO ELECTRIC, INC.
1200 W. Artesia Blvd.
Compton, CA 90220

**JOS. SCHNEIDER & CO.
(OPTISCHE WERKE)**
Distributed in USA by:
Tele-Cine, Inc., Inc.
5434 Merrick Rd.
Massapequa, NY 11758

SCHUDEL, INC.
6973 Consolidated Way
San Diego, CA 92121

SENNHEISER ELECTRONICS
10 W. 37 St.
New York, NY 10018

SHARP ELECTRONICS CORP.
(Div. of Sharp Corp., Japan)
PO Box 588
10 Keystone Pl.
Paramus,NJ 07652

SHINTRON CO., INC.
144 Rogers St.
Cambridge, MA 02142

SHURE BROTHERS
222 Hartley Ave.
Evanston, IL 60204

**SINGER EDUCATION
SYSTEMS**
(Div. of Singer Co.)
3750 Monroe Ave.
Rochester, NY 14603

**SKIRPAN LIGHTING
CONTROL CORP.**
61-03 32 Ave.
Woodside, NY 11377

**SMITH-MATTINGLY PRO-
DUCTIONS, LTD.**
2560 Huntington Ave., Suite 303
Alexandria, VA 22303

**SMITH-VICTOR SALES
CORP.**
301 N. Colfax St.
Griffith, IN 46319

SONAR RADIO CORP.
3000 Stirling Rd.
Hollywood,FL 33021

**SONY VIDEO PRODUCTS
CO.**
(Div. of Sony Corp. of America)
9 W. 57 St.
New York, NY 10019

SPECTRA-VISION CORP.
1528 Belfield Ave.
Philadelphia, PA 19141

STOREEL CORP.
PO Box 80523
2050C Carroll Ave., Suite #2
Atlanta, GA 30341

STRAND CENTURY, INC.
(Div. of Rank Industries America)
20 Bushes Lane
Elmwood Park, NJ 07407

SYSTEMS CONCEPTS, INC.
395 Ironwood Dr.
Salt Lake City, UT 84115

TANDON DIVISION
(Div. of United Ventures, Inc.,
River Forest, IL)
2323 H Bluemound Rd.
Waukesha, WI 53186

TAPEMAKER
48 Urban Ave.
Westbury, NY 11590

TDK ELECTRONICS CORP.
755 Eastgate Blvd.
Garden City, NY 11530

TEKTRONIX, INC.
PO Box 500
Beaverton, OR 97077

**TELEDYNE CAMERA
SYSTEMS**
(Div. of Teledyne Industries, Inc.)
1901 Ave. of the Stars
Los Angeles, CA 90067

TELEMATION
(Div. of Bell & Howell,
Chicago, IL)
PO Box 15068
Salt Lake City, UT 84115

TELESCRIPT, INC.
20 Insley St.
Demarest, NJ 07627

**TELEVISION EQUIPMENT
ASSOCIATES**
PO Box 260
South Salem, NY 10590

**TELEVISION PRODUCTS
CO., INC.**
9016 Aviation Blvd.
Inglewood, CA 90301

**TELEVISION RESEARCH
INTERNATIONAL (TRI)**
1003 Elwell Court
Palo Alto, CA 94303

TELE VUE OPTICS, INC.
15 Green Hill Lane
Spring Valley, NY 10977

TENTEL CORP.
50 Curtner Ave.
Campbell, CA 95008

**THALNER ELECTRONIC
LABORATORIES, INC.**
7235 Jackson Rd.
Ann Arbor, MI 48103

**THERMODYNE INTER-
NATIONAL LTD.**
12600 Yukon Ave.
Hawthorne, CA 90250

**THOMSON-CSF ELECTRON
TUBES**
(Div. of Thomson-CSF, France)
750 Bloomfield Ave.
Clifton, NJ 07015

**TIFFEN MANUFACTURING
CORP.**
90 Oser Ave.
Hauppauge, NY 11787

TIMES WIRE AND CABLE CO.
(Div. of Times Fiber Communications)
358 Hall Ave.
Wallingford, CT 06492

TOTAL VIDEO SUPPLY CO.
9060 Clairemont Mesa Blvd.
San Diego, CA 92123

**TROMPETER ELECTRONICS,
INC.**
8936 Comanche Ave.
Chatsworth, CA 91311

TURNER ENGINEERING, INC.
14 Morris Ave.
Mountain Lakes, NJ 07046

UNI-SET
(Div. of Kniff Woodcraft Corp.)
449 Ave. A
Rochester, NY 14621

**UNIVEX INTERNATIONAL,
LTD.**
Box 2000
Monument, CO 80132

U.S. JVC CORP.
(Subs. of Victor Co. of Japan)
58-75 Queens Midtown Expwy.
Maspeth, NY 11378

UTAH SCIENTIFIC, INC.
2276 S. 2700 W.
Salt Lake City, UT 84119

VAMCO ENGINEERING, INC.
11104 E. 56 St.
Tulsa, OK 74145

VIDEO AIDS CORP. OF COLORADO
325 E. Seventh St.
Loveland, CA 80537

VIDEO AUTOMATION SYSTEMS INC.
PO Box 21A
Route 1
Pound Ridge, NY 10576

VIDEO DATA SYSTEMS
(Div. of Sterling Television Presentation, Inc.)
40 Oser Ave.
Hauppauge, NY 11787

VIDEODETICS CORP.
1335 S. Claudina St.
Anaheim, CA 92805

VIDEOMEDIA, INC.
250 N. Wolfe Rd.
Sunnyvale, CA 94086

THE VIDEO TAPE CO.
10545 Burbank Blvd.
North Hollywood, CA 91601

VIDEO TECHNIQUES, INC.
101 W. 57 St., Suite 9K
New York, NY 10019

VIDEO TECHNOLOGY, INC.
14424 N.W. Seventh Ave.
Miami, FL 33168

VIDEOTEK, INC.
125 N. York St.
Pottstown, PA 19464

VITAL INDUSTRIES, INC.
3700 N.E. 53 Ave.
Gainesville,FL 32601

VULCAN BINDER & COVER
(Div. of EBSCO, Birmingham, AL)
Box 29
Vincent, AL 35178

WELT/SAFE-LOCK, INC.
2400 W. Eighth Lane
Hialeah, FL 33010

WILLIAM BAL CORP.
947 Newark Ave.
Elizabeth, NJ 07208

THE WINSTED CORP.
8127 Pleasant Ave. S.
Minneapolis, MN 55420

WOLF COACH, INC.
200 Bartlett St.
Northboro, MA 01532

WORLD VIDEO INC.
PO Box 117
23 S. Reading Ave.
Boyerstown, PA 19512

ZEI-MARK CORP.
PO Box 182
Brookfield Center, CT 06805

Index

Other Titles from Knowledge Industry Publications

Videotext: The Coming Revolution in Home/Office Information Retrieval
edited by Efrem Sigel
154 pages   hardcover $24.95

The Executive's Guide to TV and Radio Appearances
by Michael Bland
144 pages   hardcover $14.95

Practical Video: The Manager's Guide to Applications
by John A. Bunyan, James C. Crimmins and N. Kyri Watson
203 pages   softcover $17.95

The Video Register, 1980-81 edition
250 pages (approx.)   softcover $34.95

Television and Management: The Manager's Guide to Video
by John A. Bunyan and James C. Crimmins
154 pages   hardcover $17.95

Video in the Classroom: A Guide to Using Creative Television
by Don Kaplan
161 pages   softcover $24.50

Viewdata and Videotext, 1980-81: A Worldwide Report
Transcript of international conference
624 pages   softcover $75.00

Video Discs: The Technology, the Markets and the Future
by Efrem Sigel, Mark Schubin, Paul Merrill, et. al.
160 pages (approx.)   hardcover $29.95

Video User's Handbook
by Peter Utz
410 pages   hardcover $19.95

Available from Knowledge Industry Publications, Inc., 2 Corporate Park Drive, White Plains, NY 10604.